I0845231

I am grateful to God for everything! And I believe that the meaning of life is to make sense of other lives. C.A., you are the meaning of my life.
Lov U

WCOUTO
2023

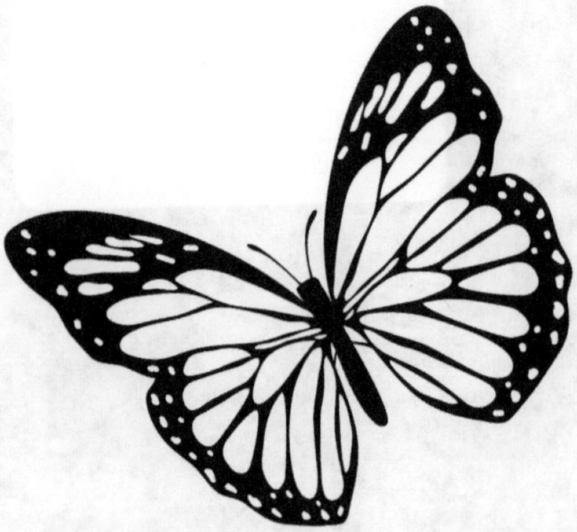
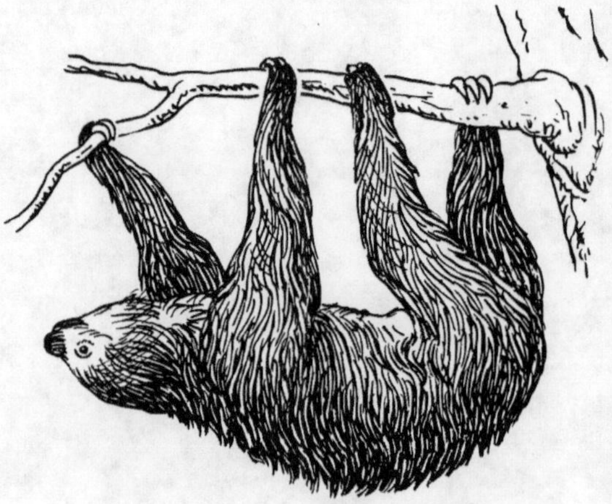

This Book Belongs to:

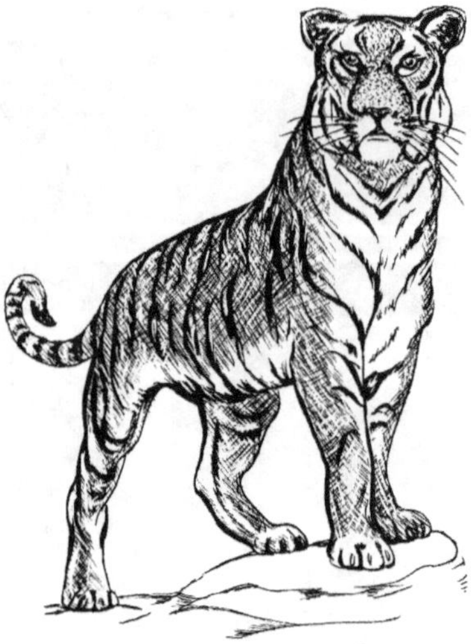
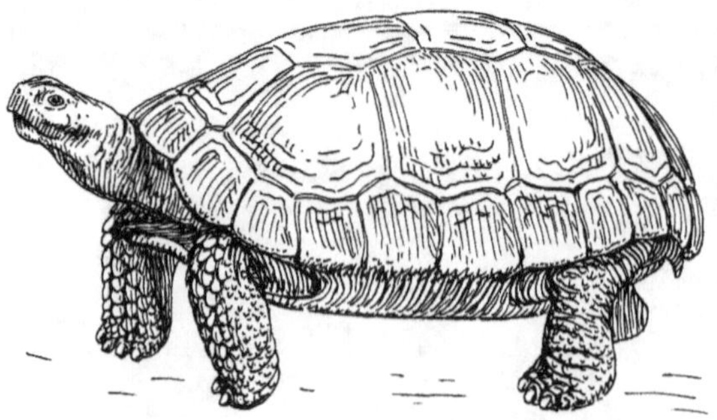

W.COUTO ©
publications

Test Color Page

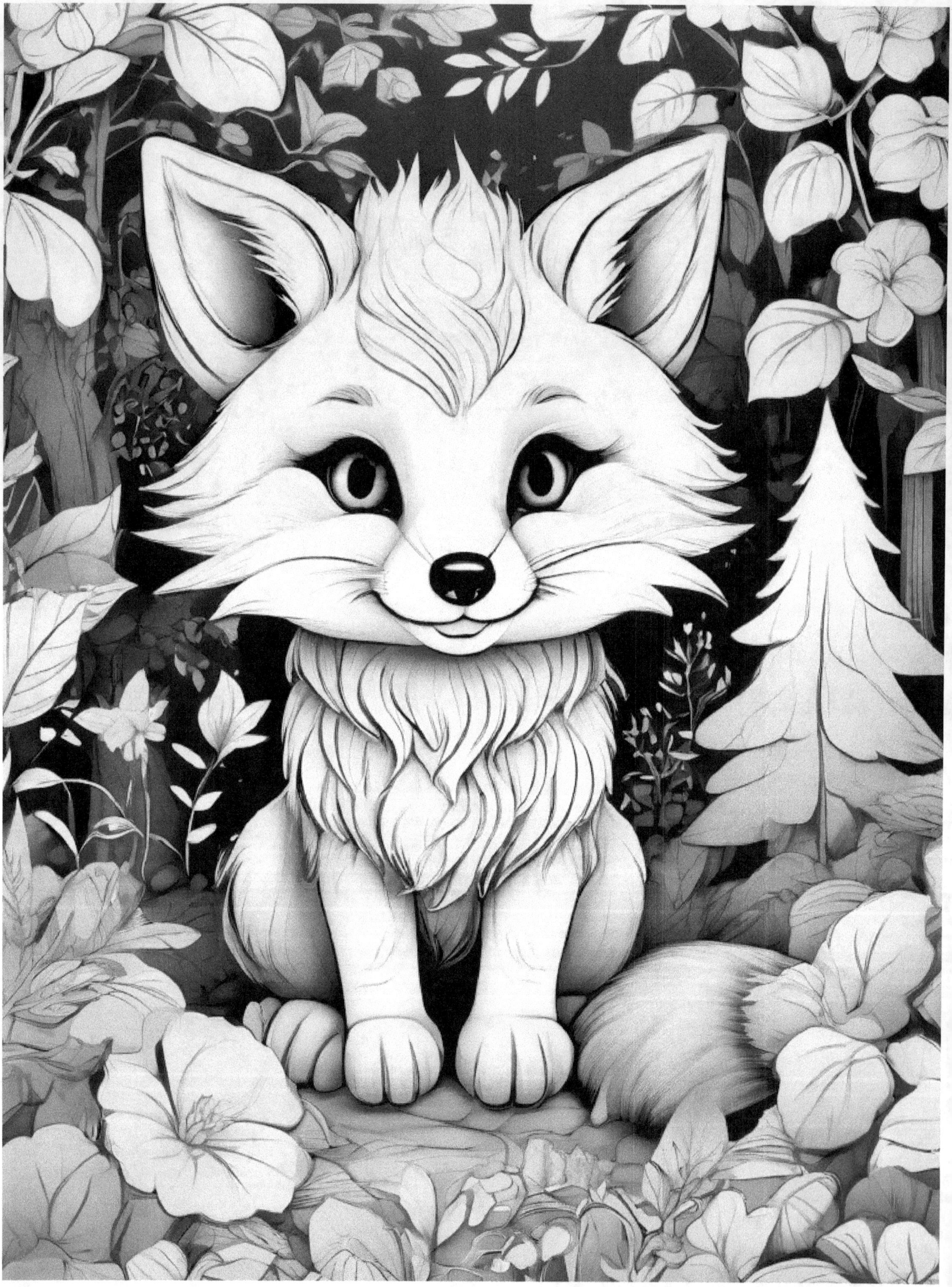

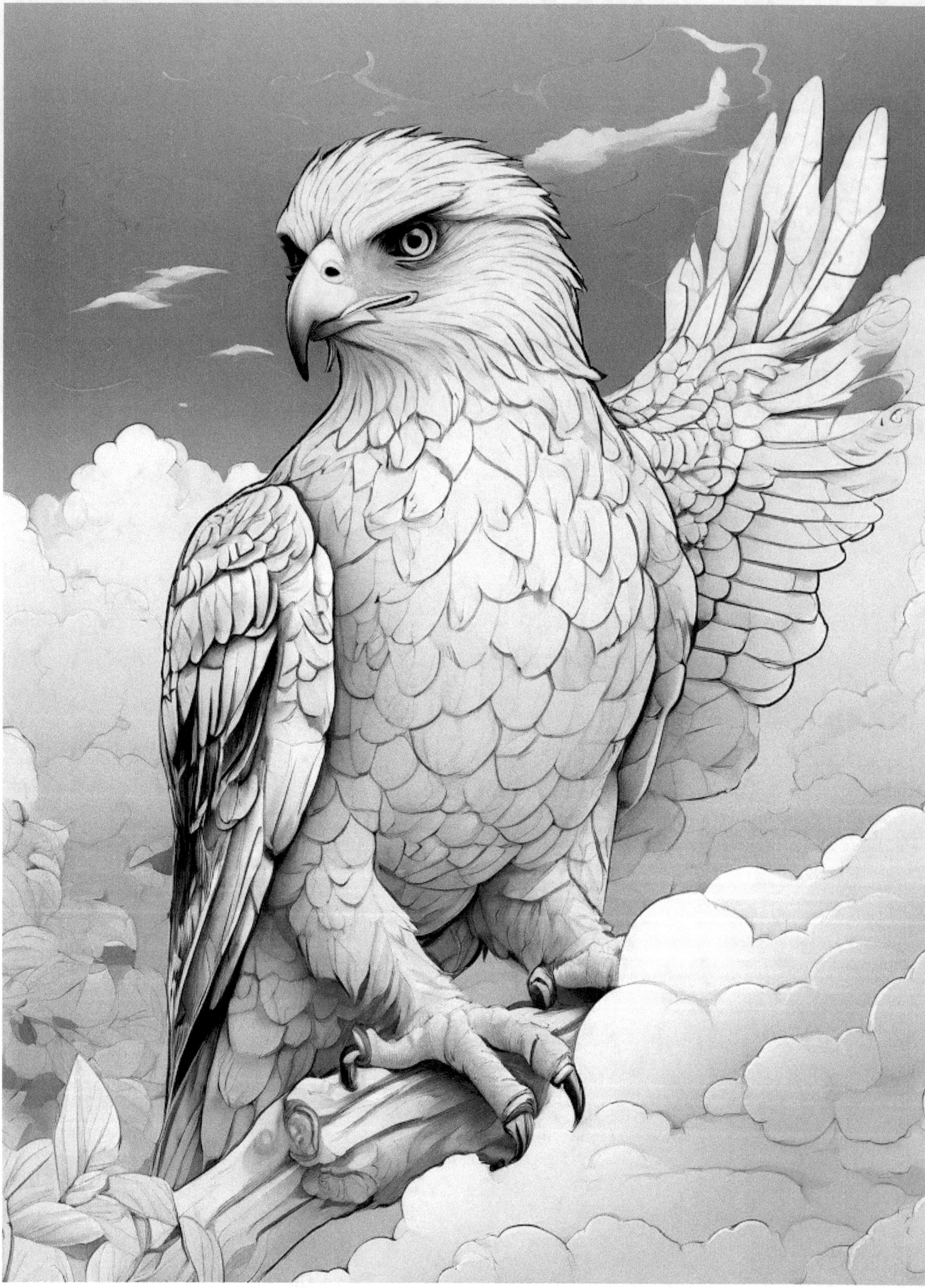

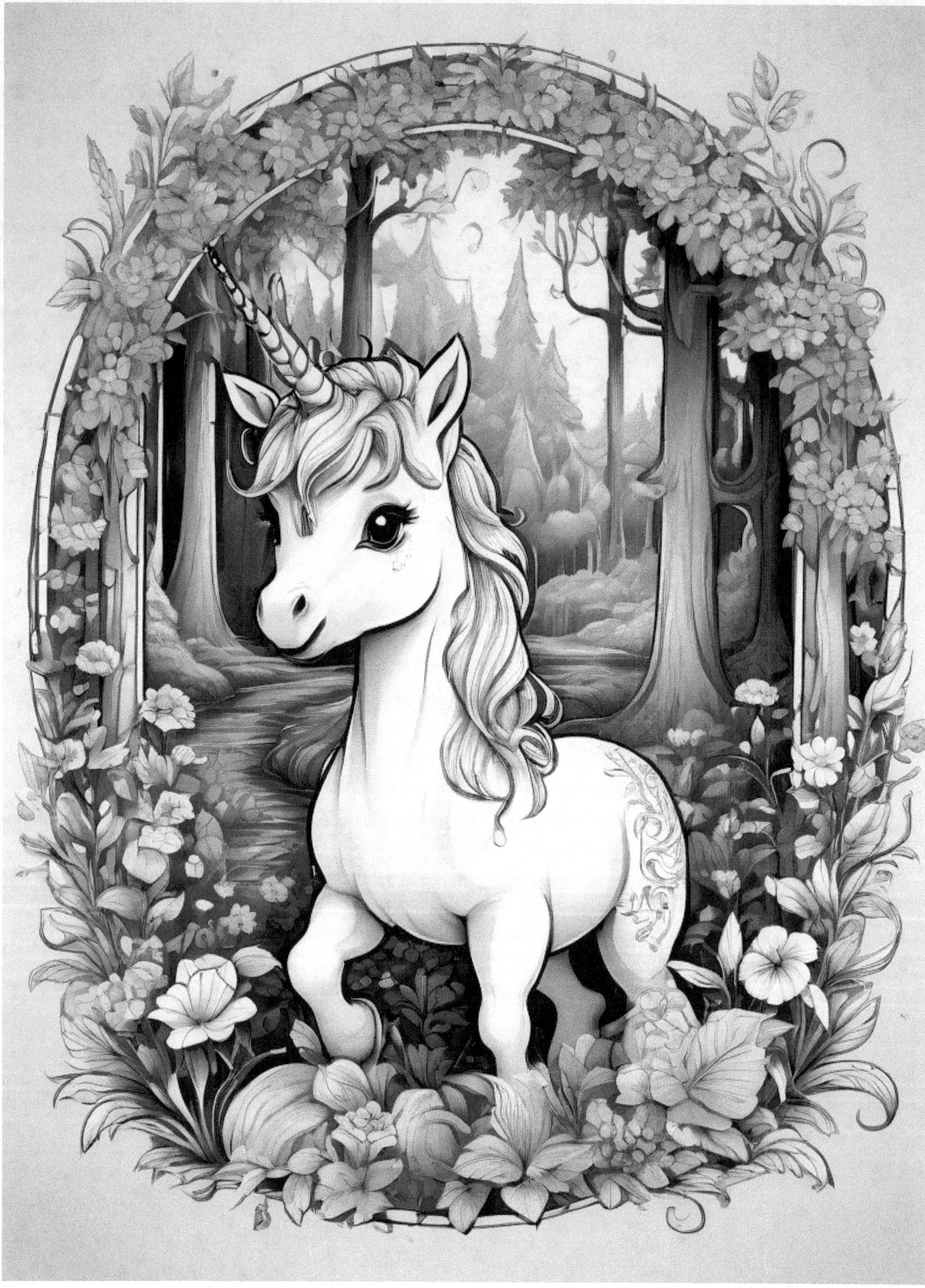

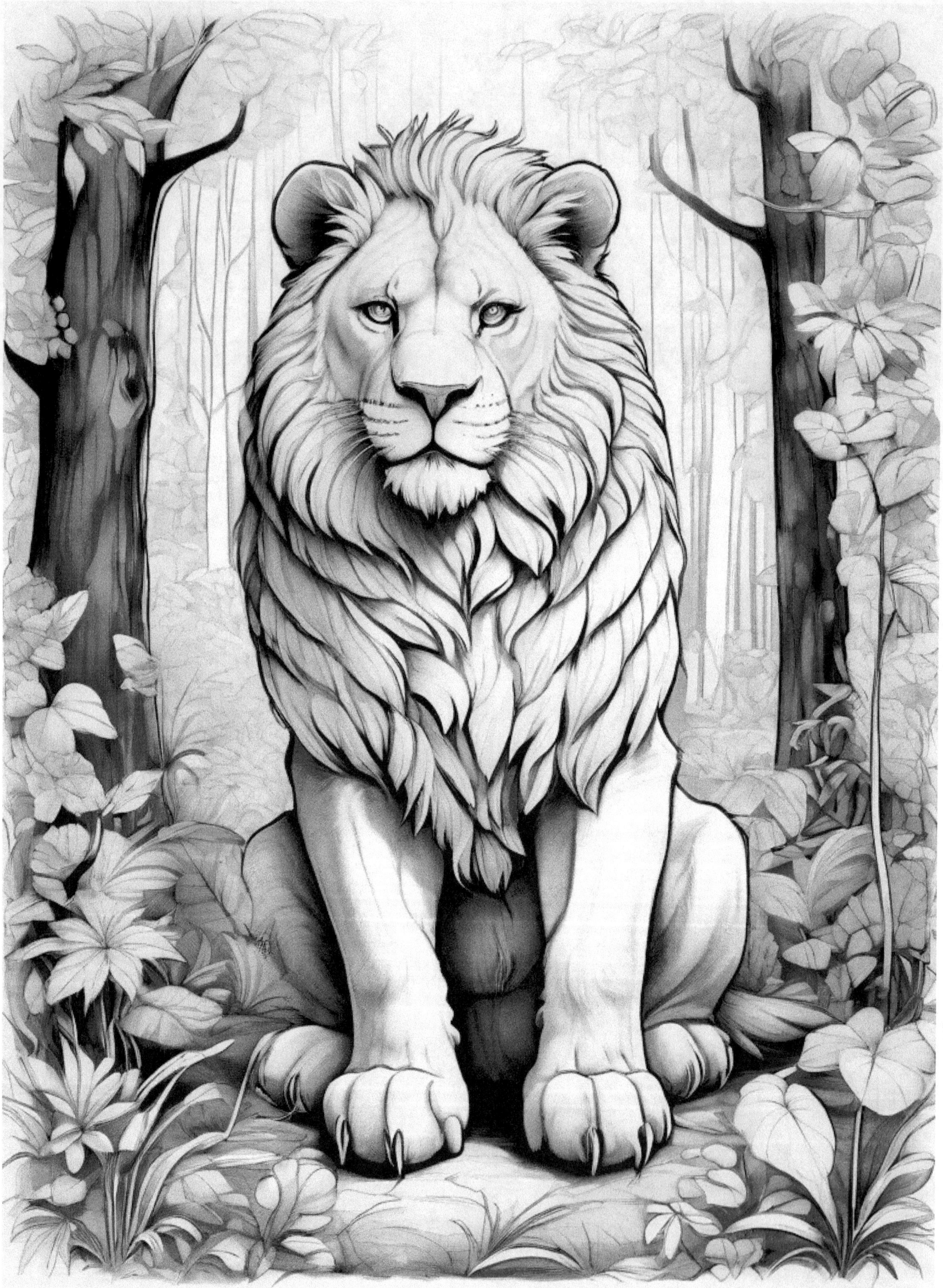

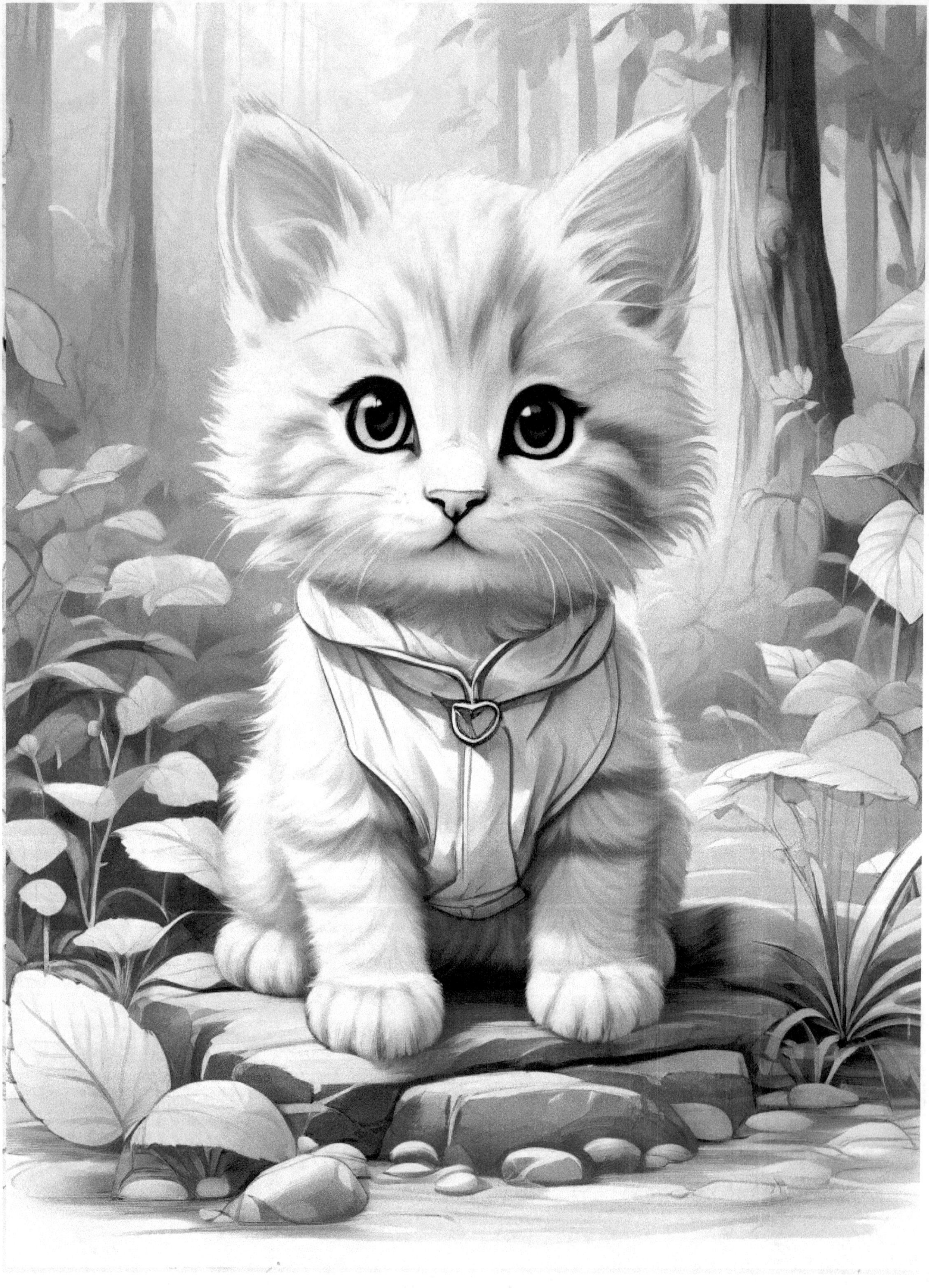

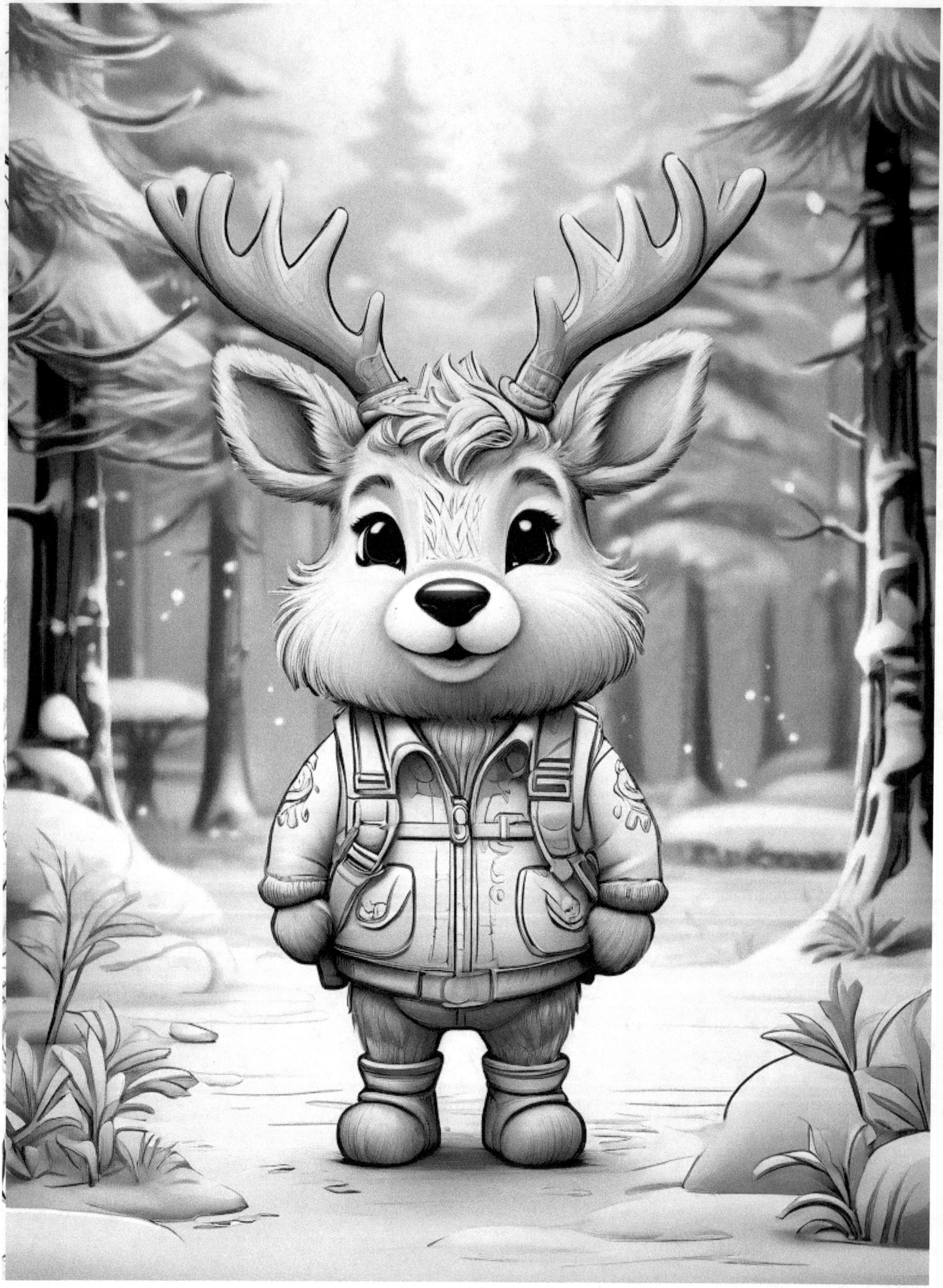

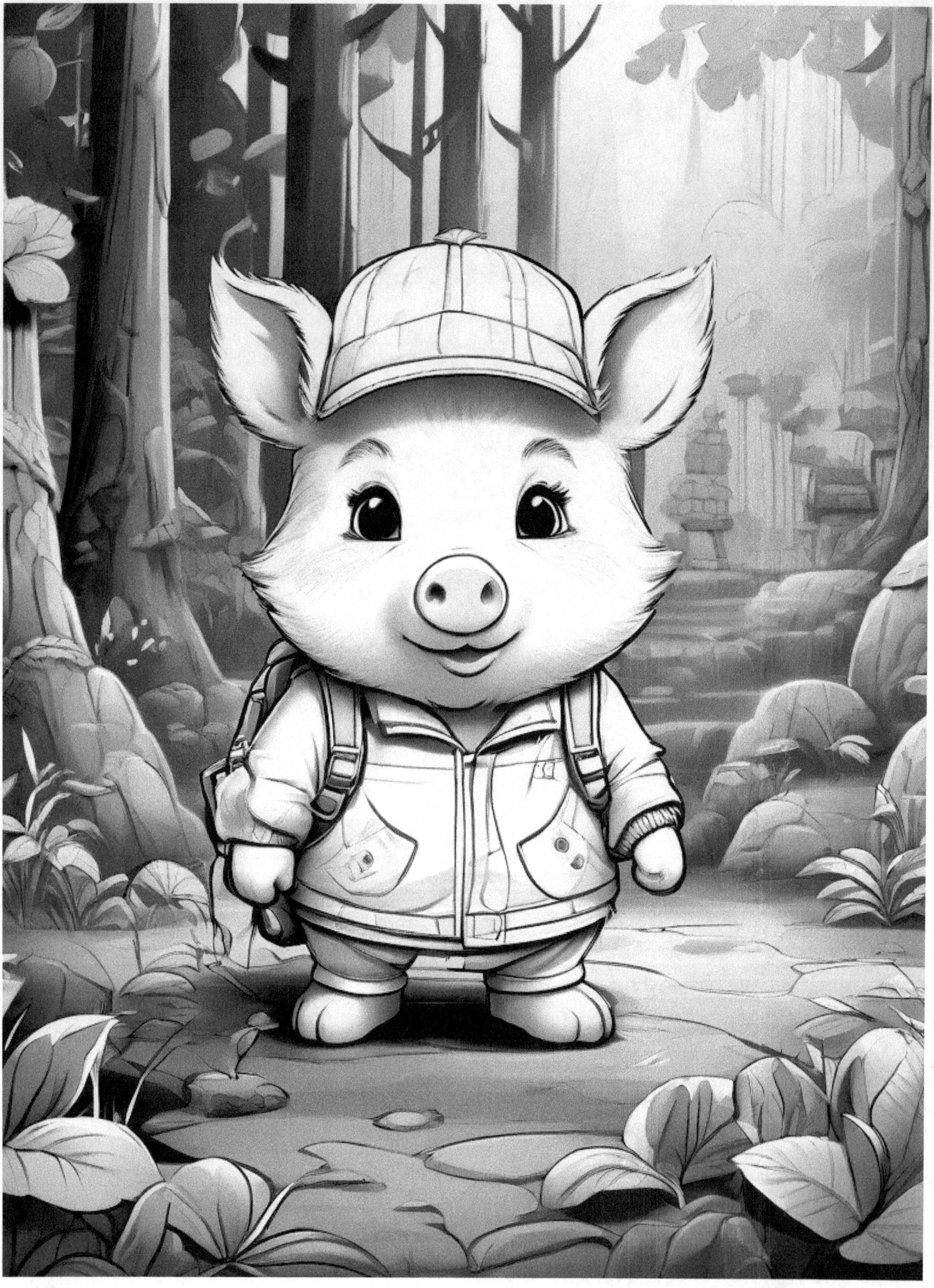

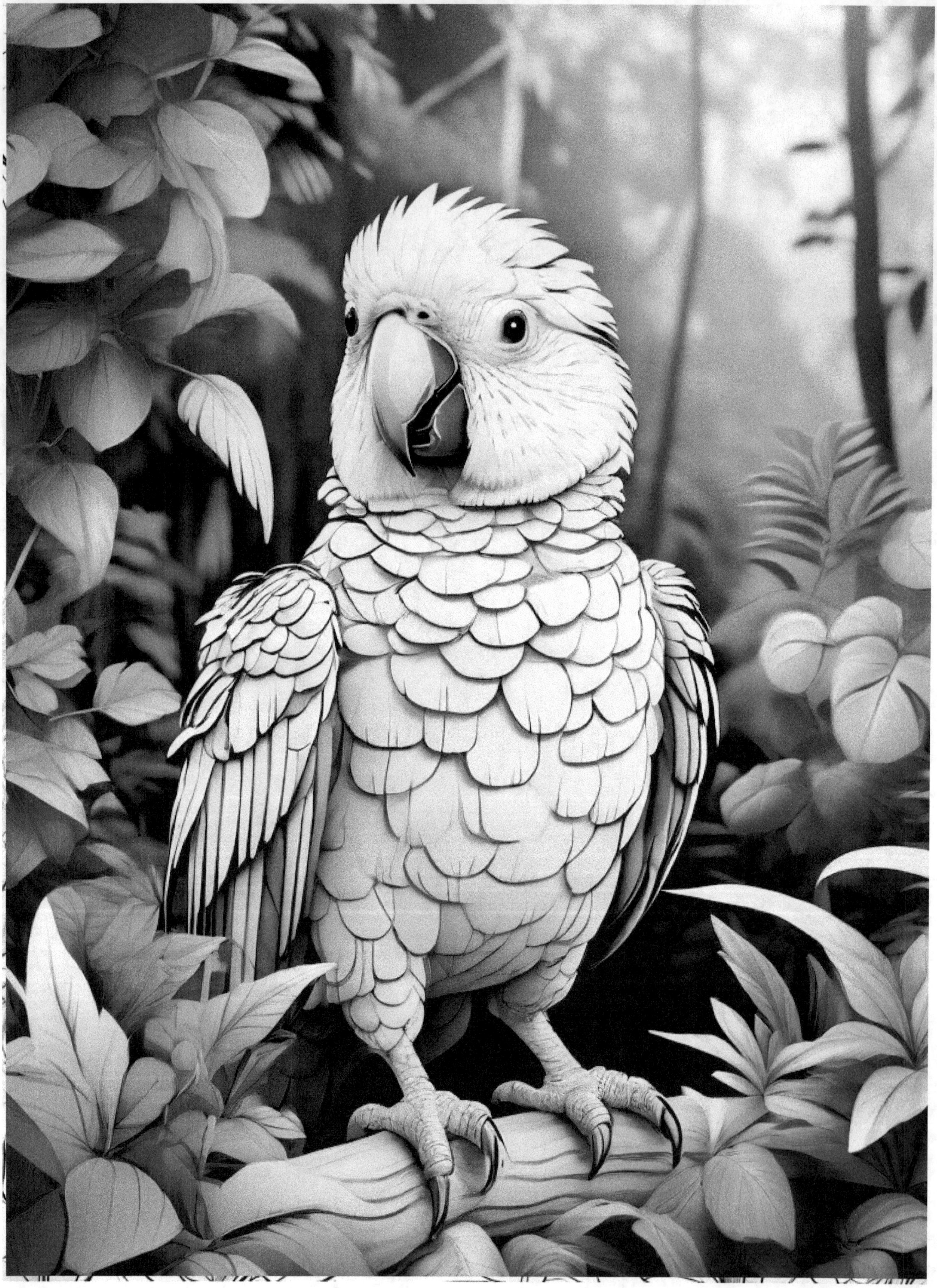

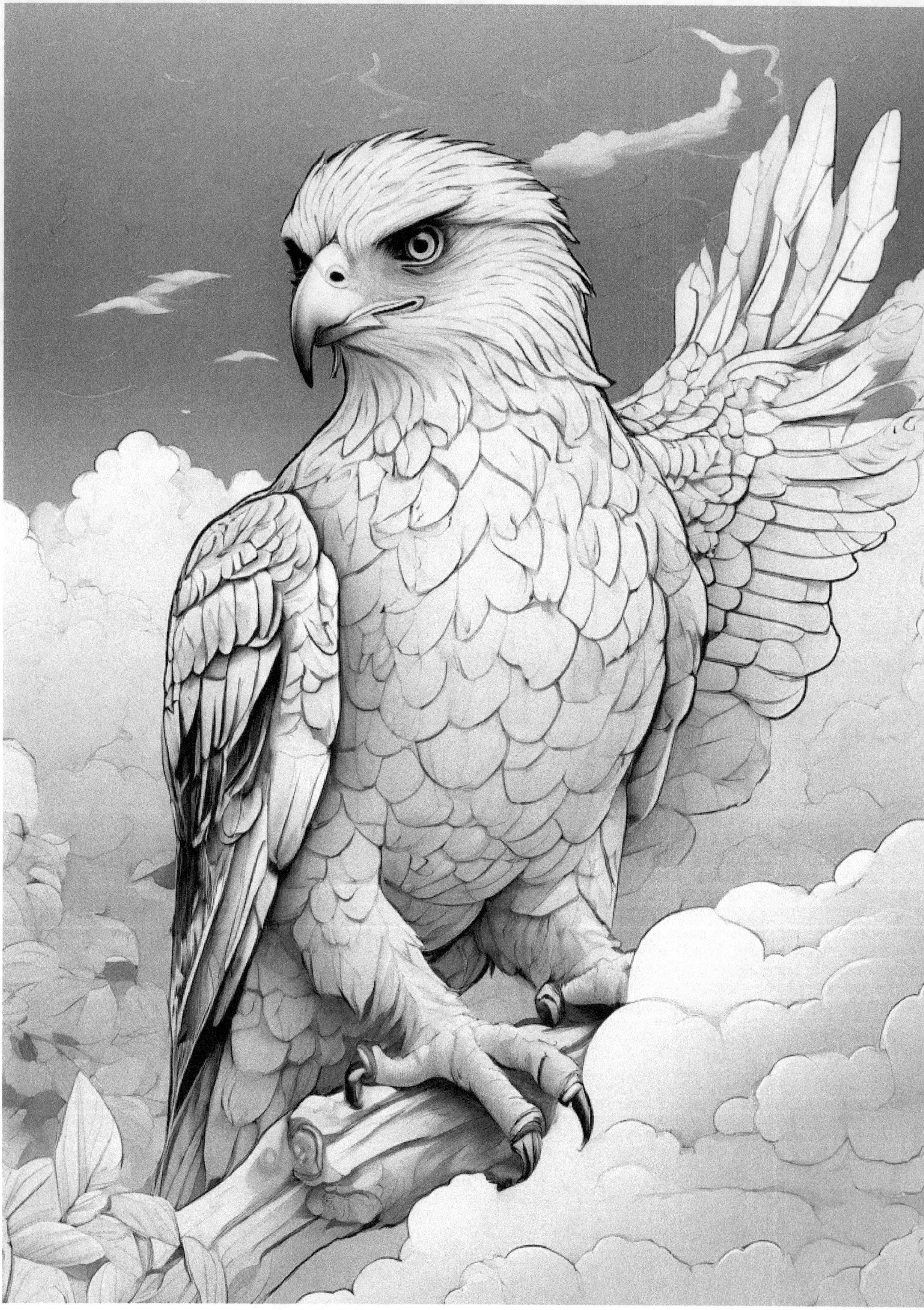

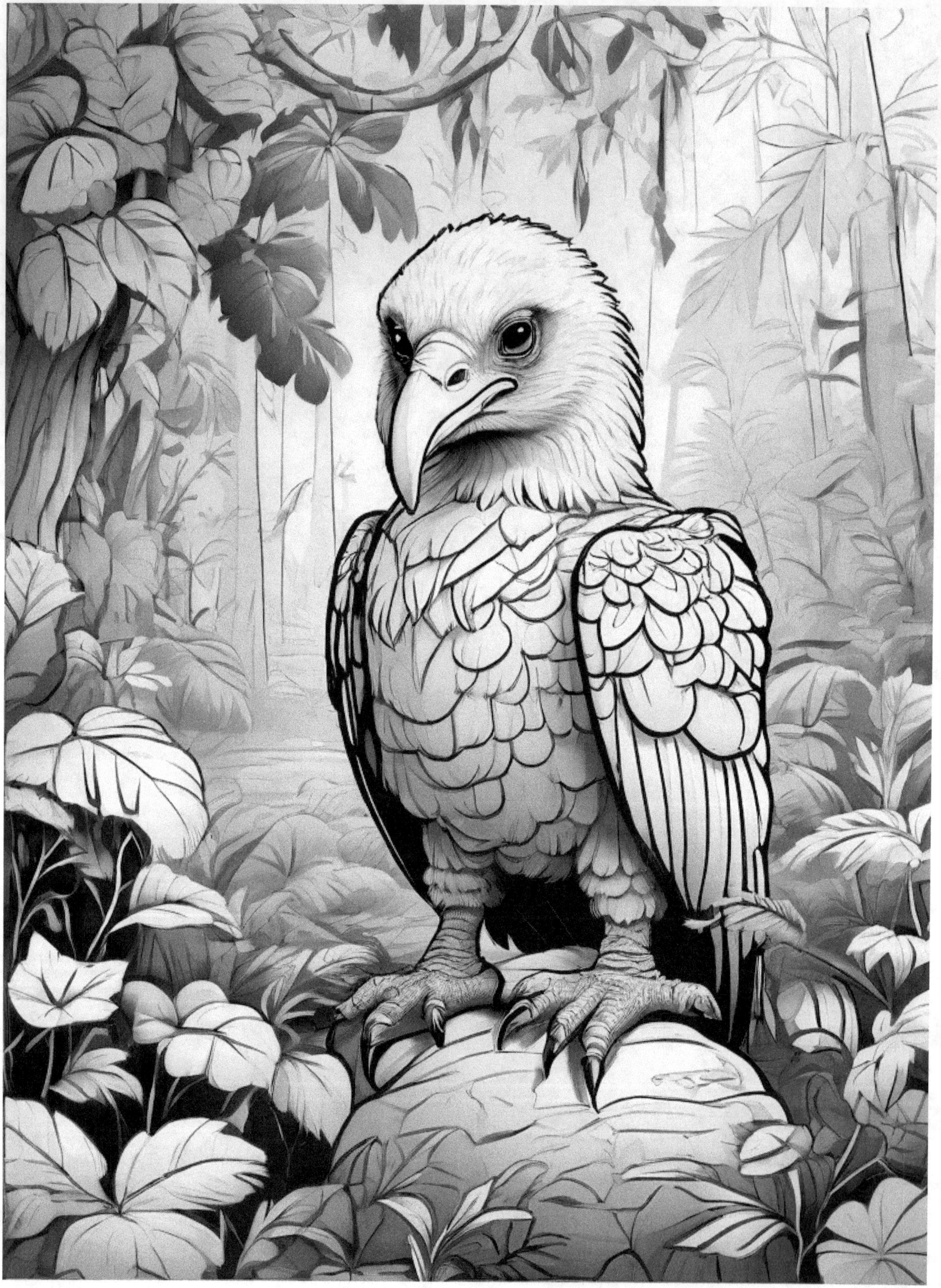

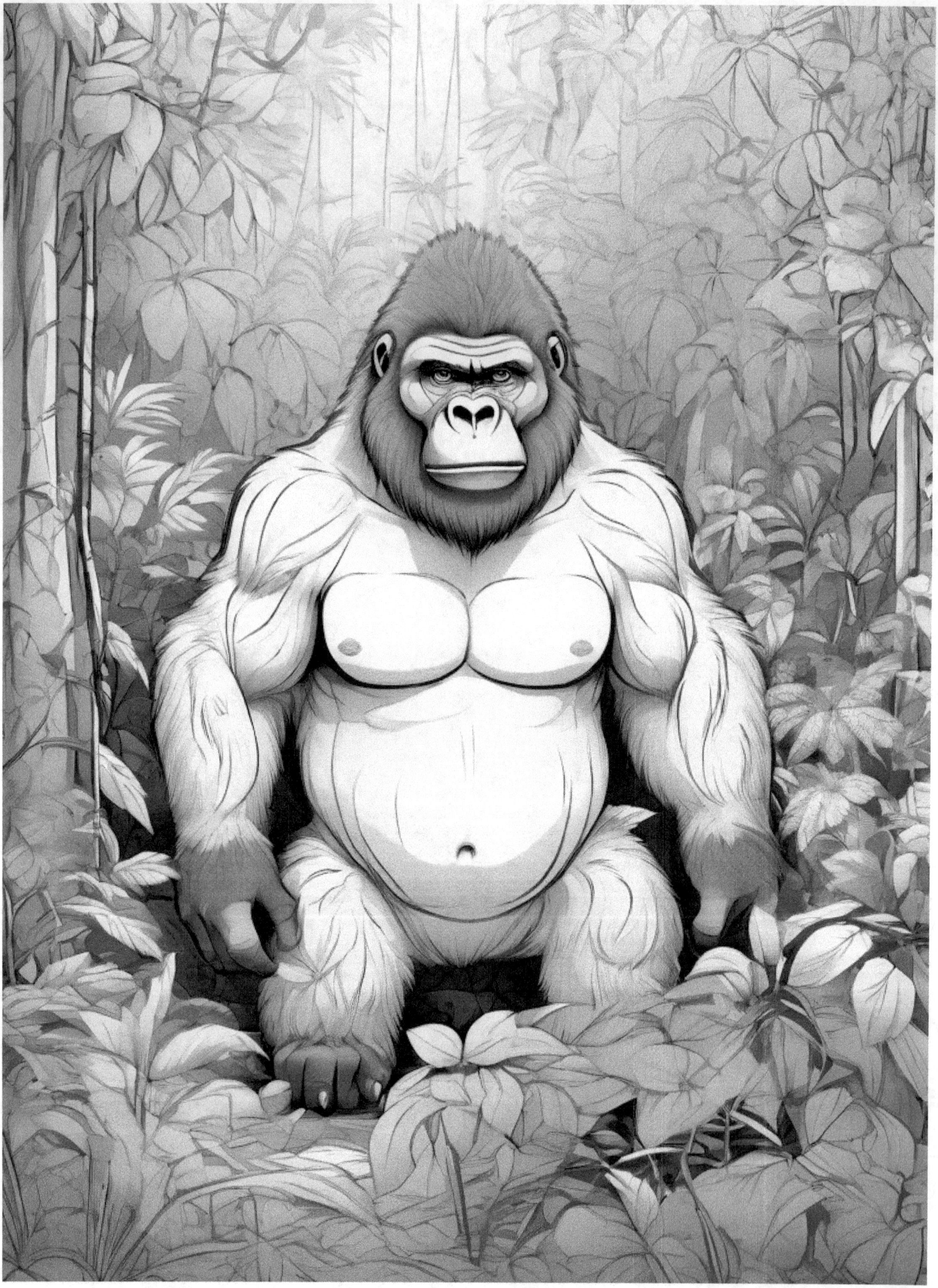

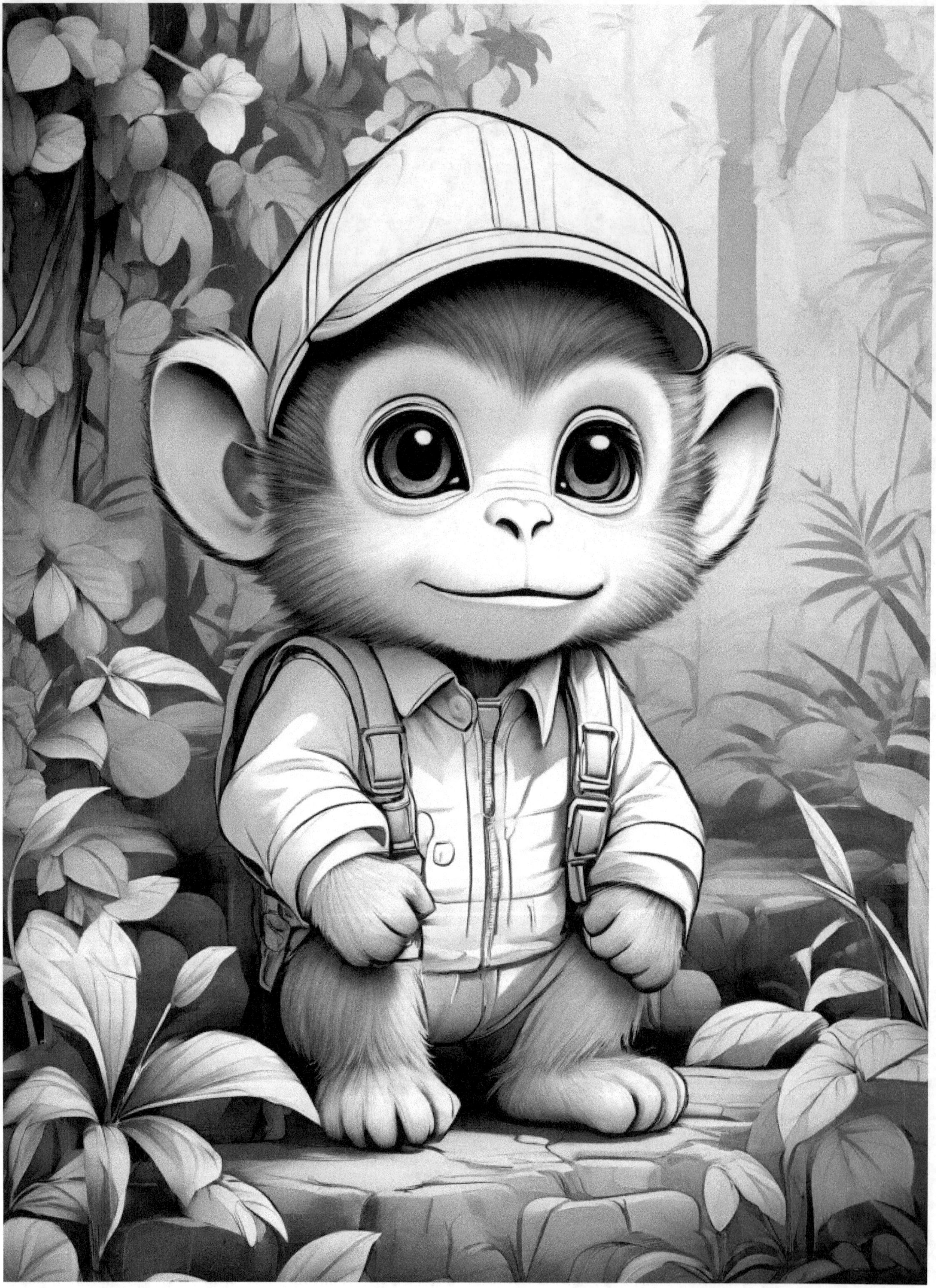

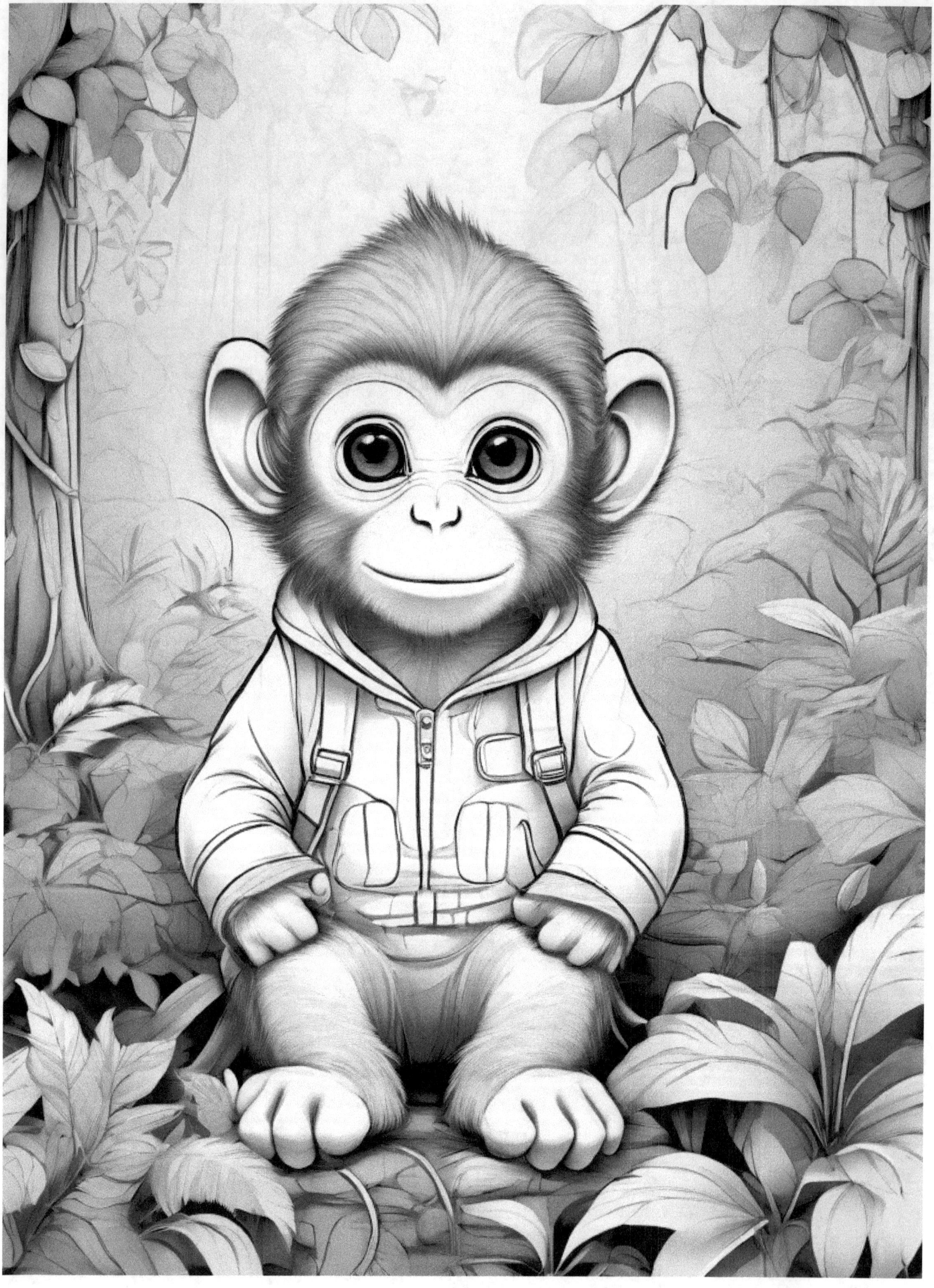

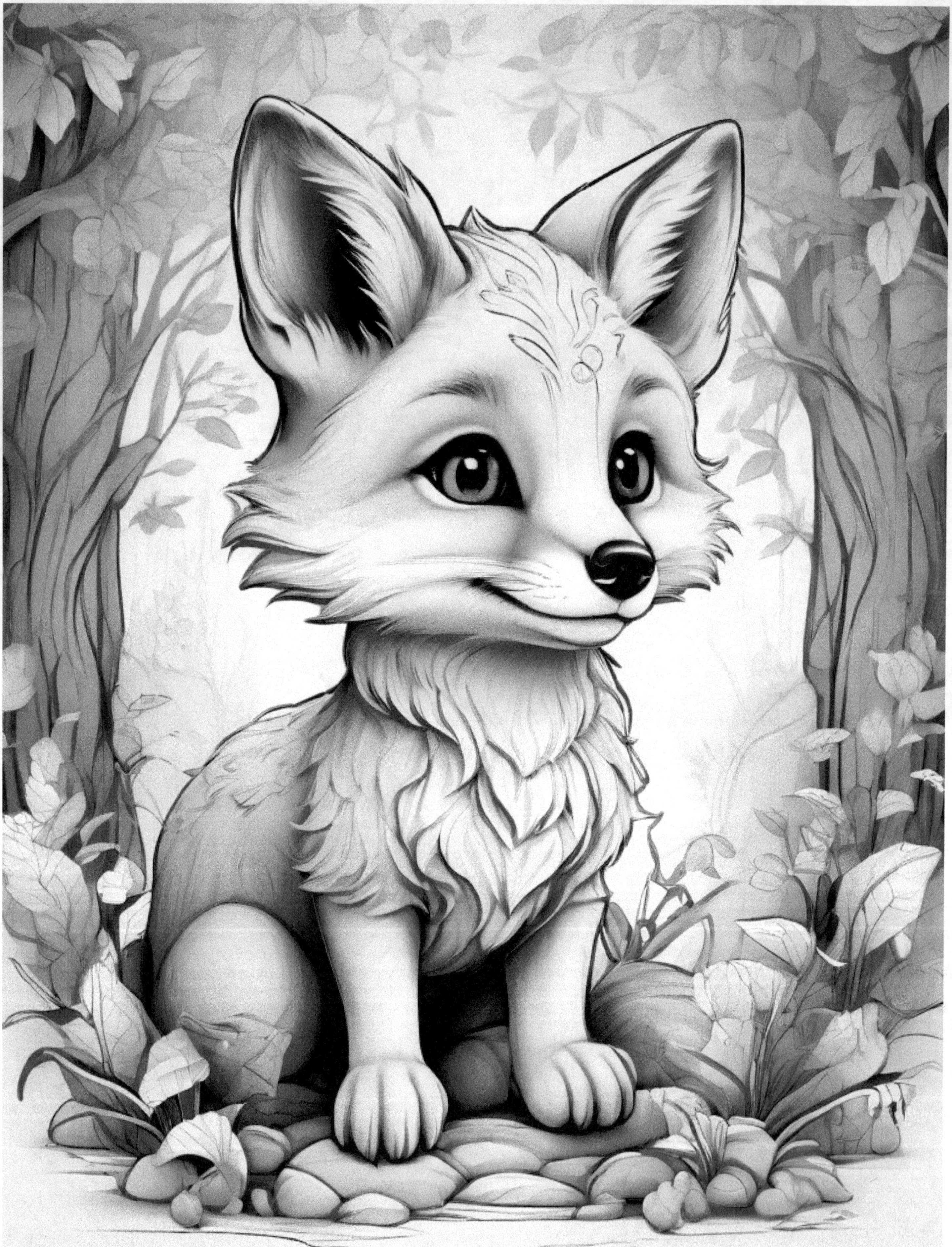

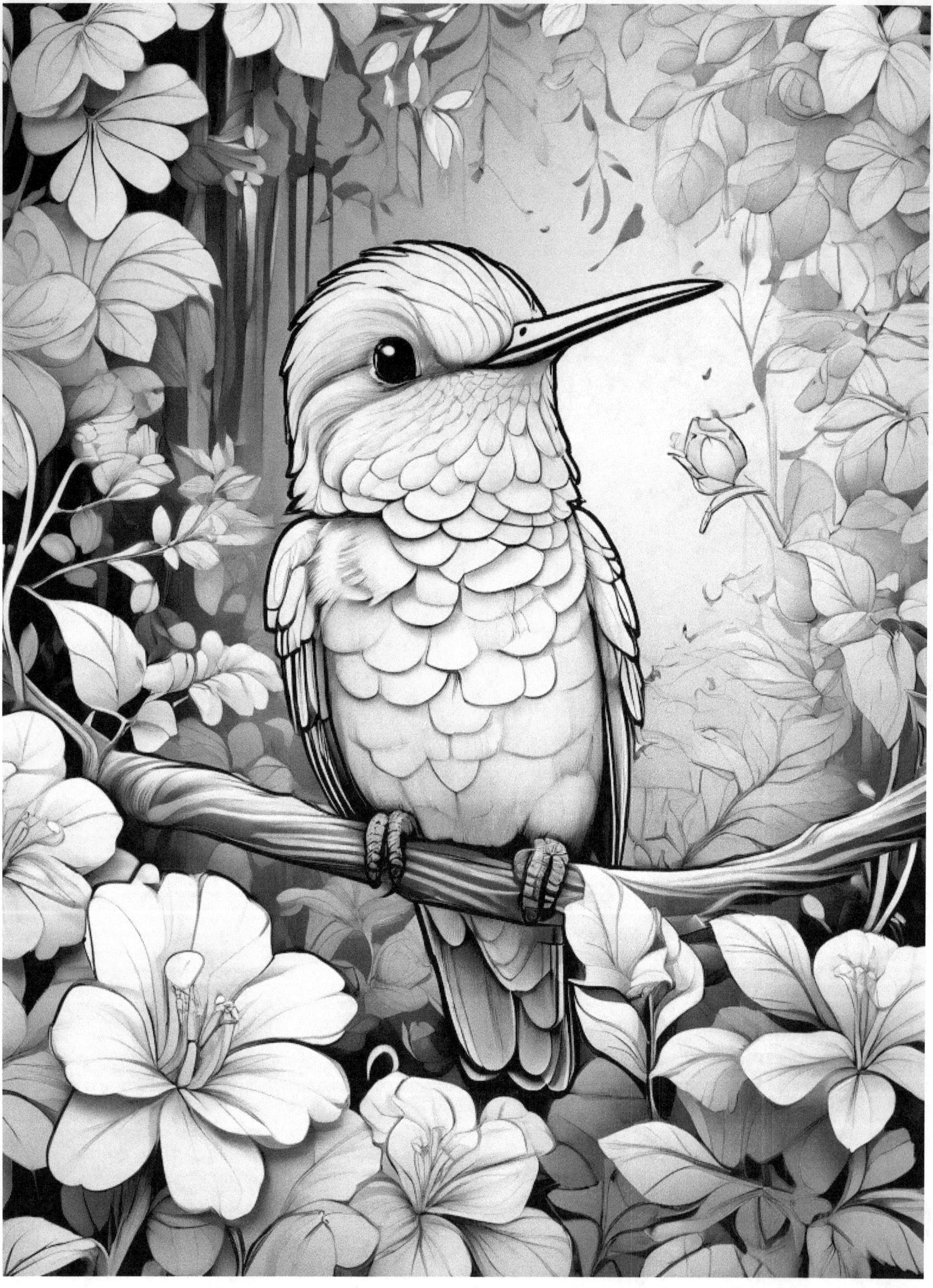

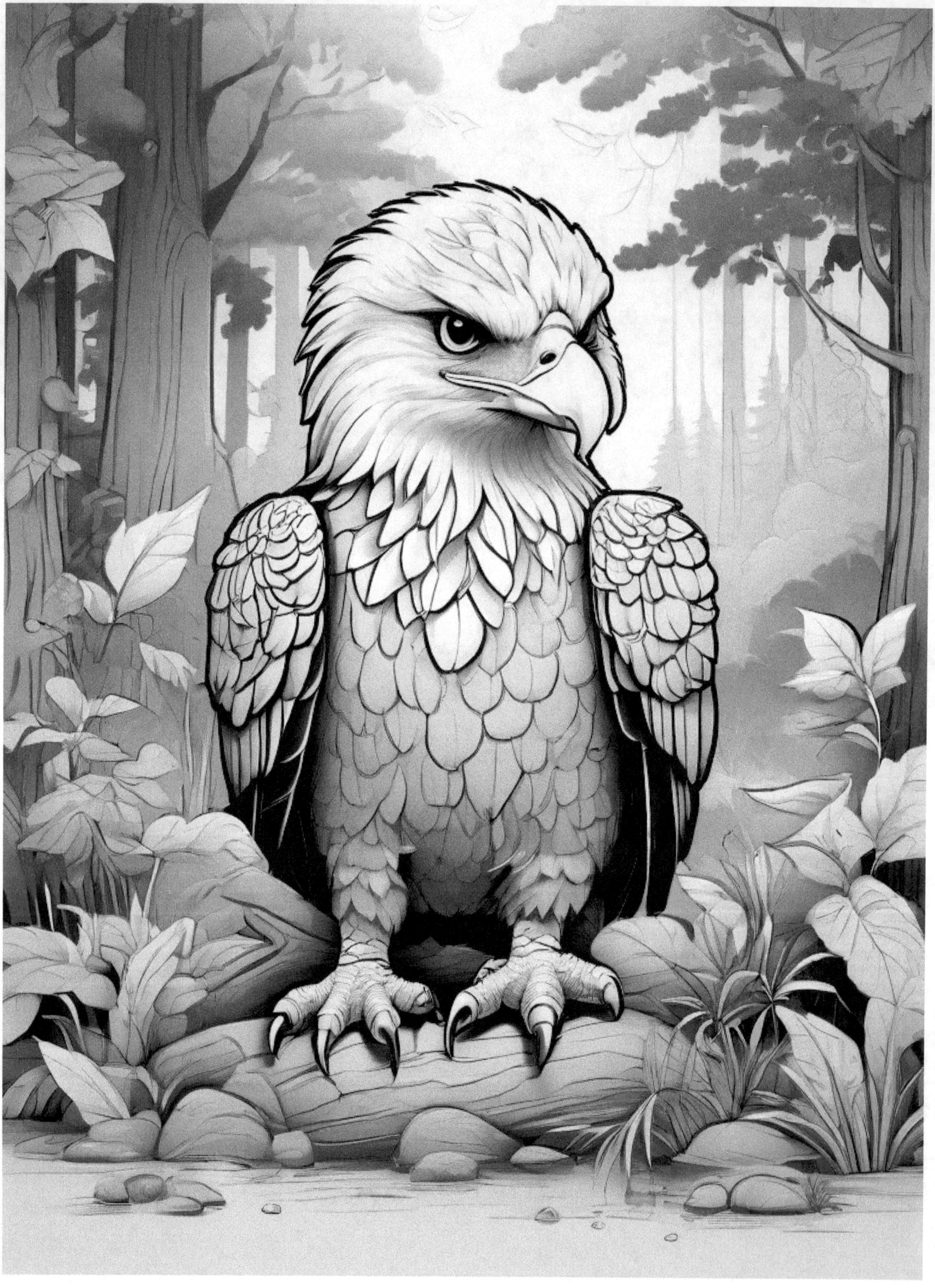

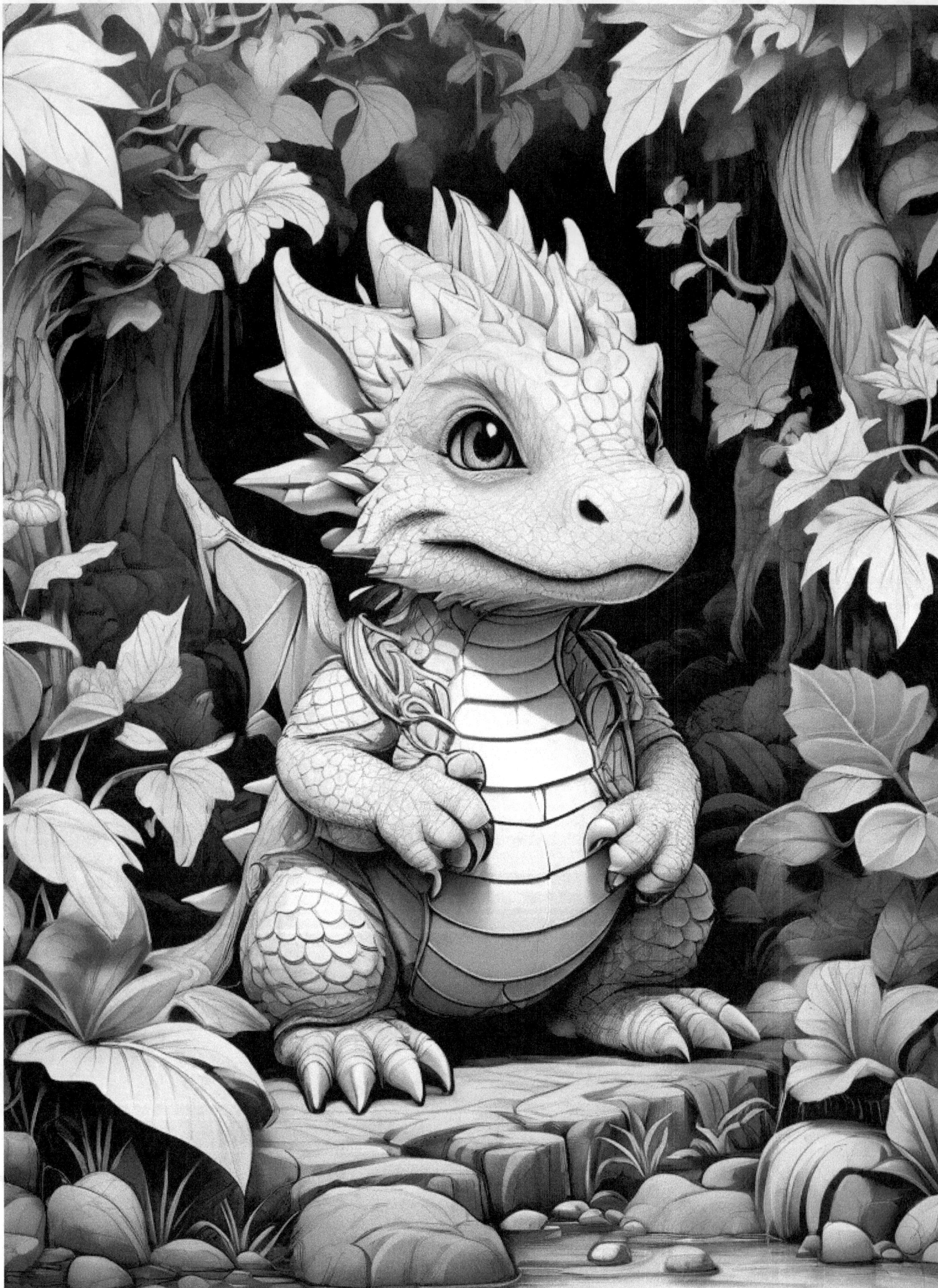

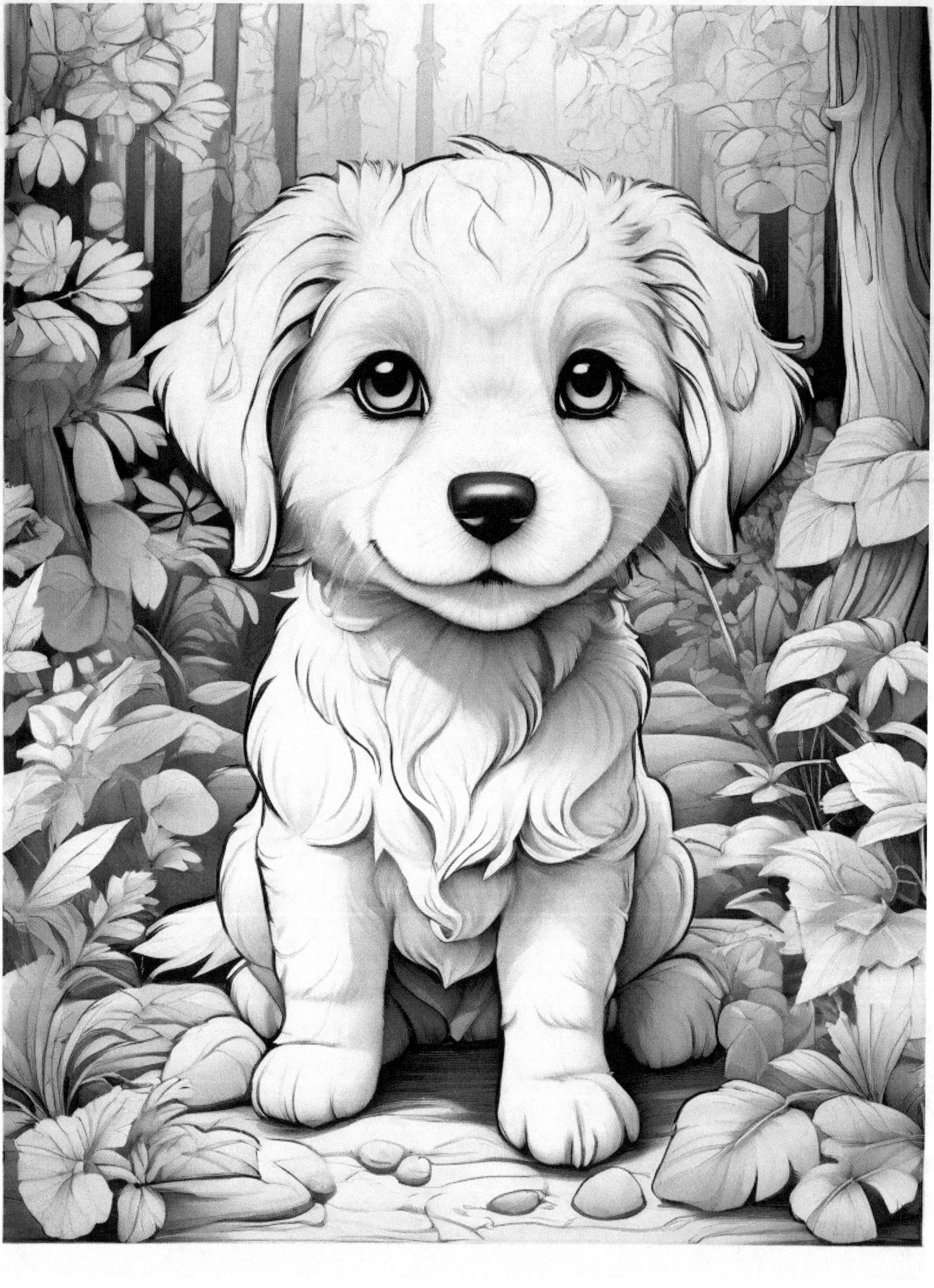

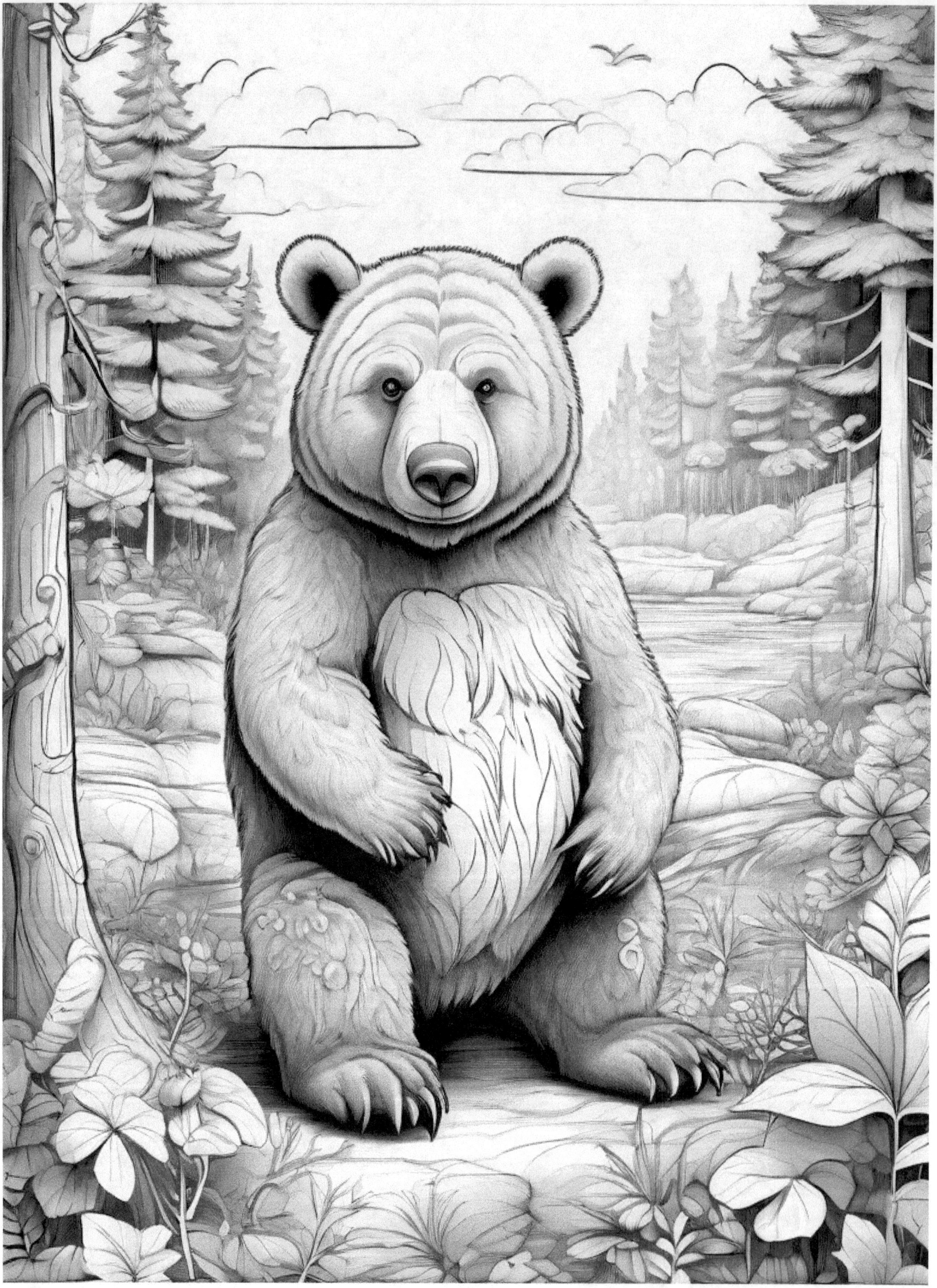

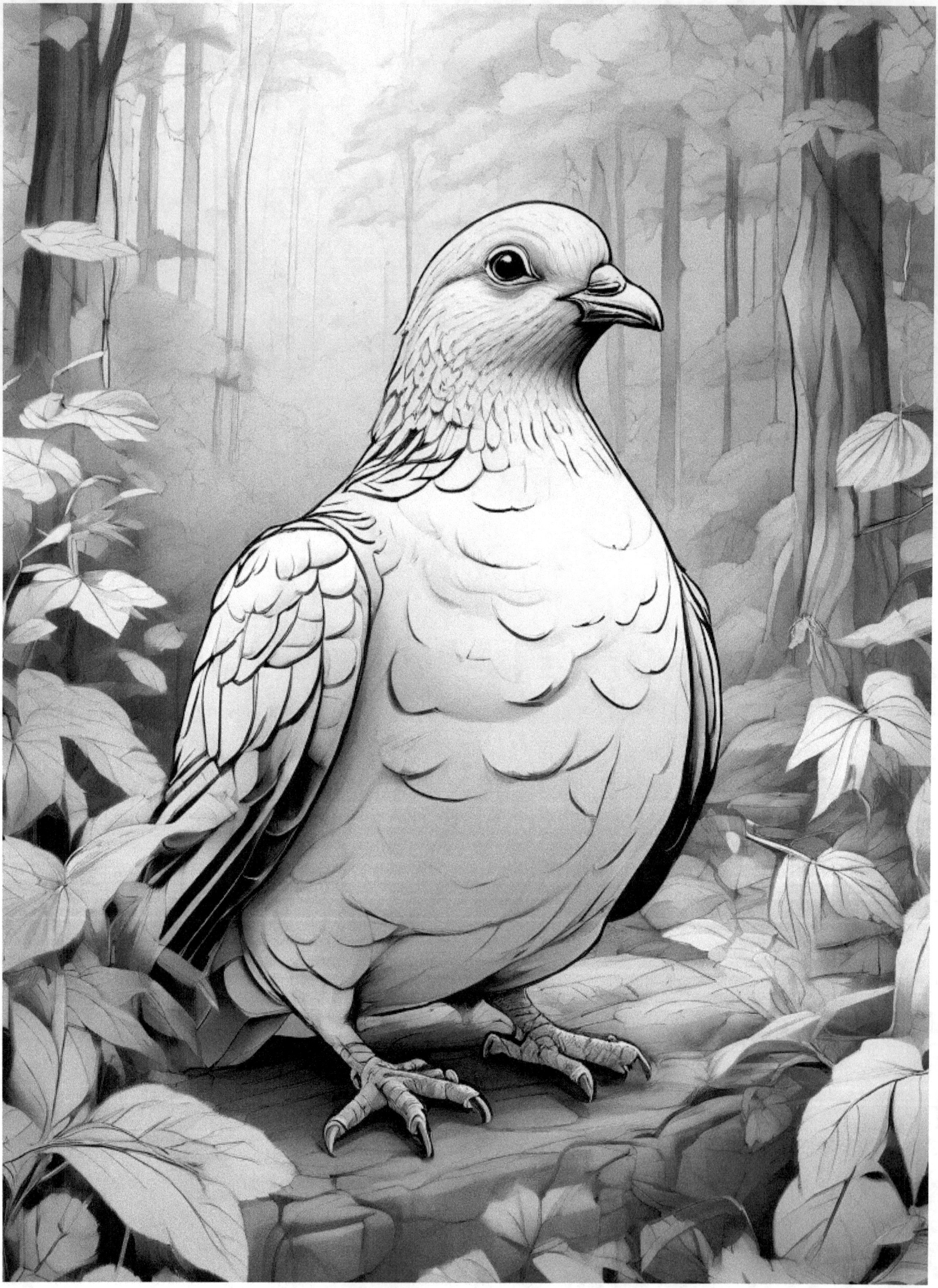

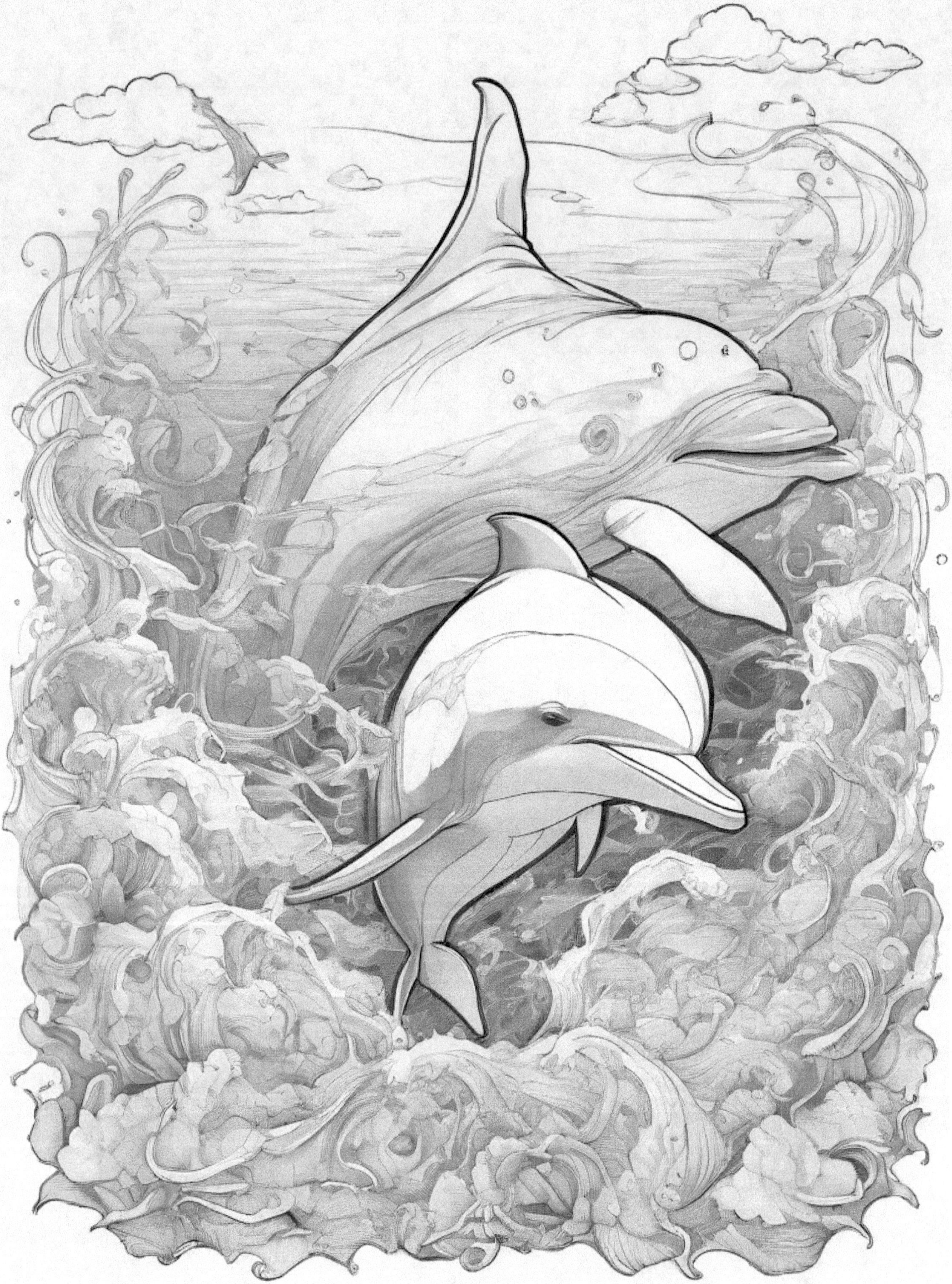

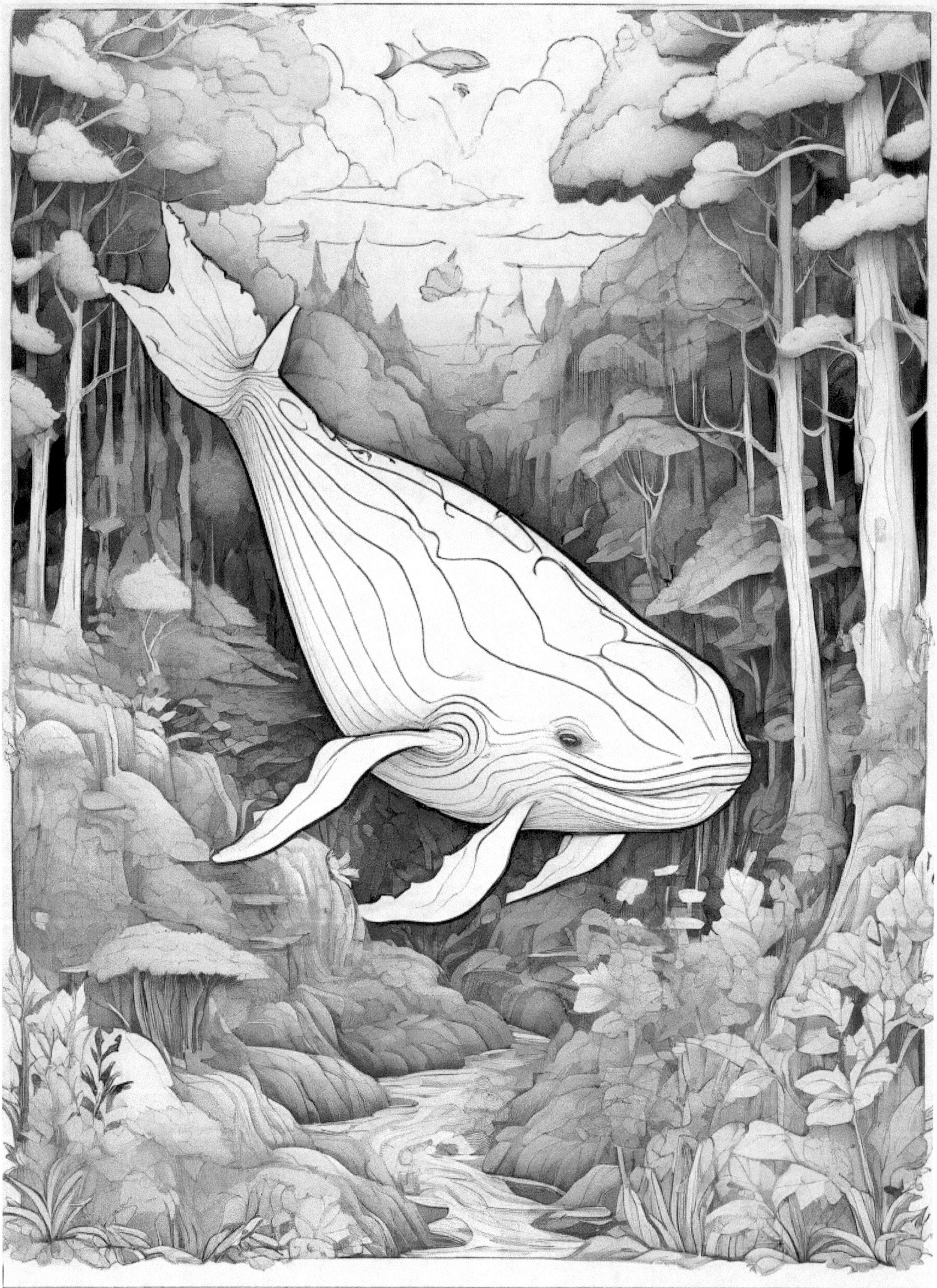

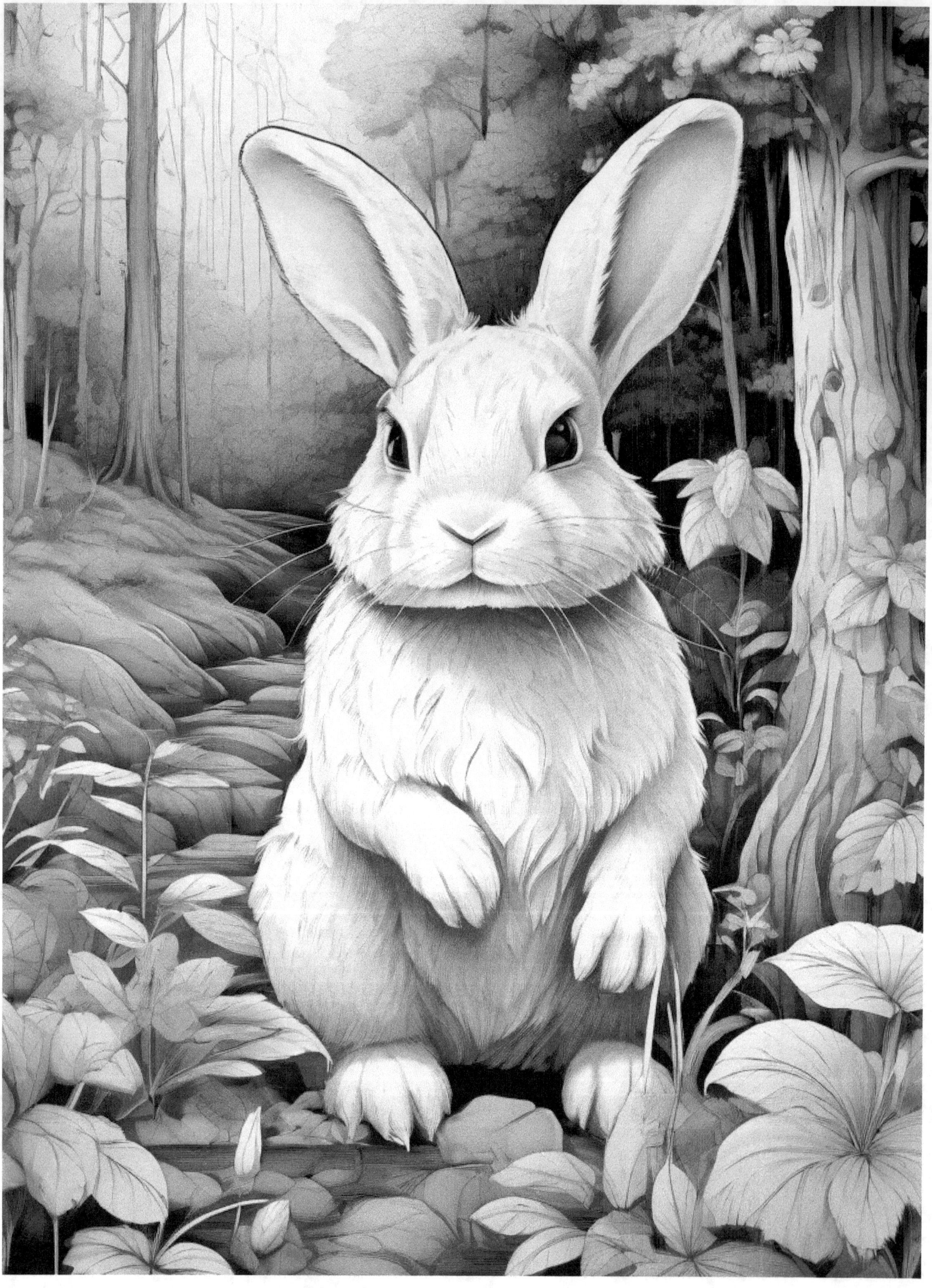

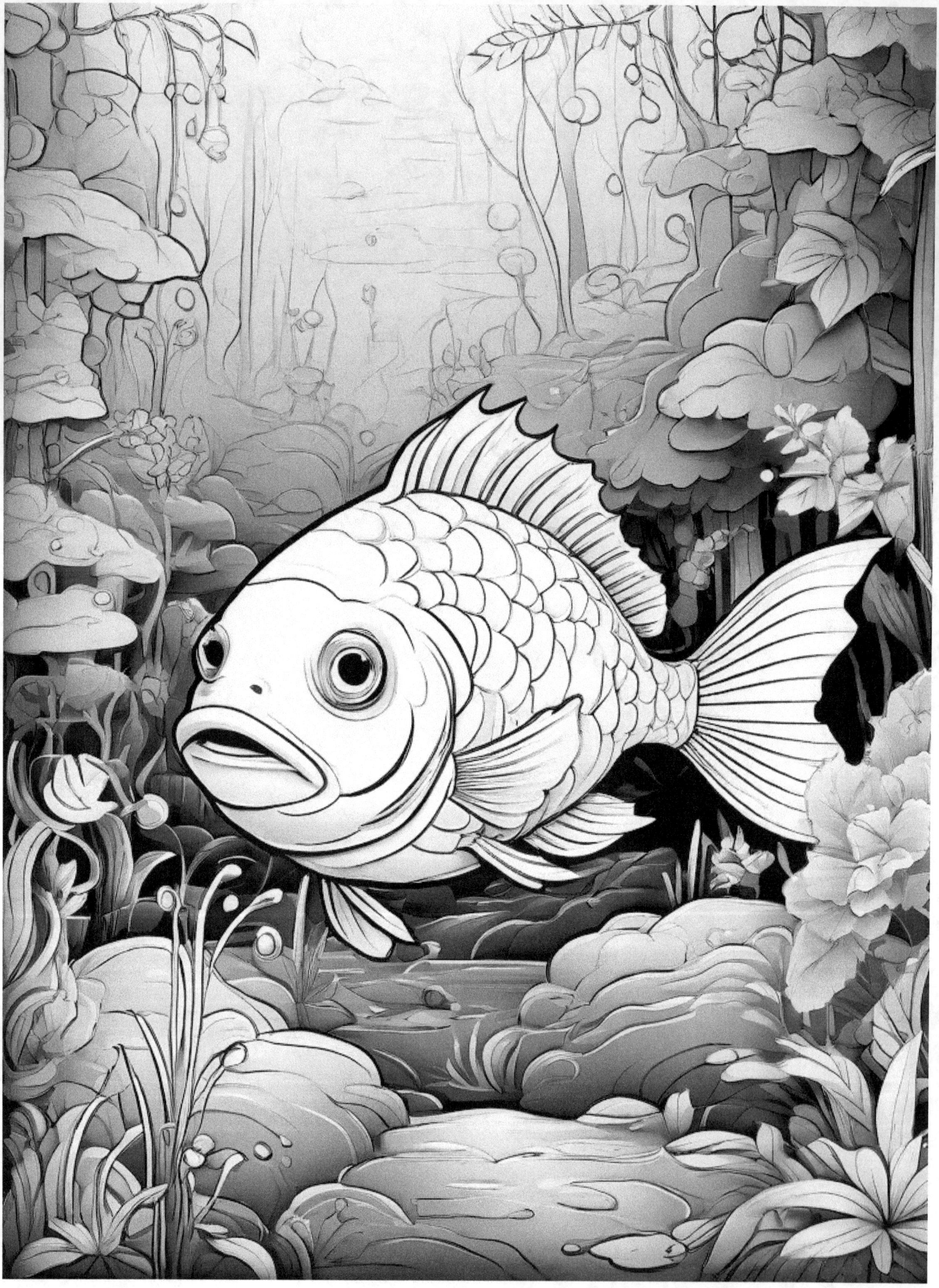

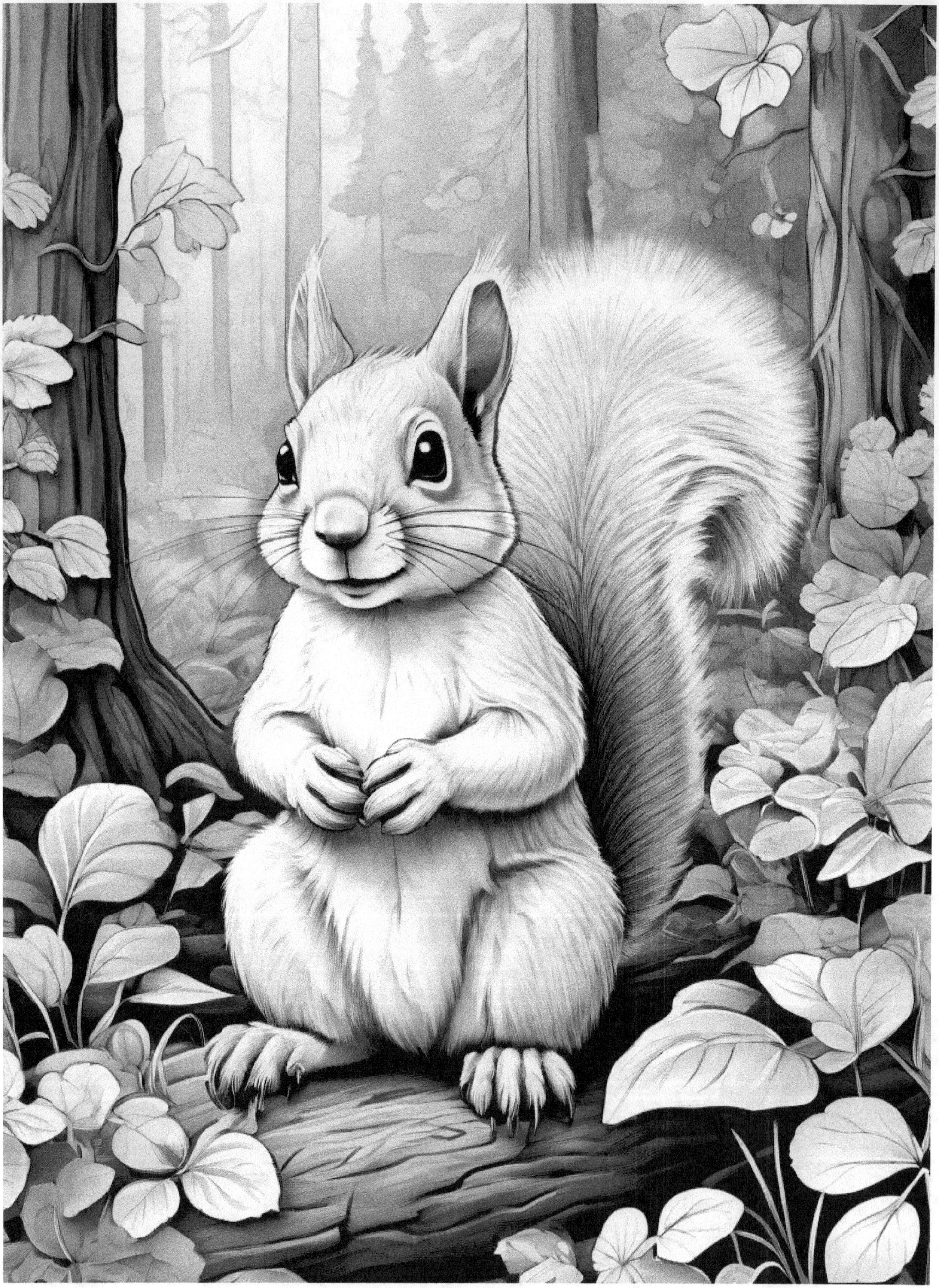

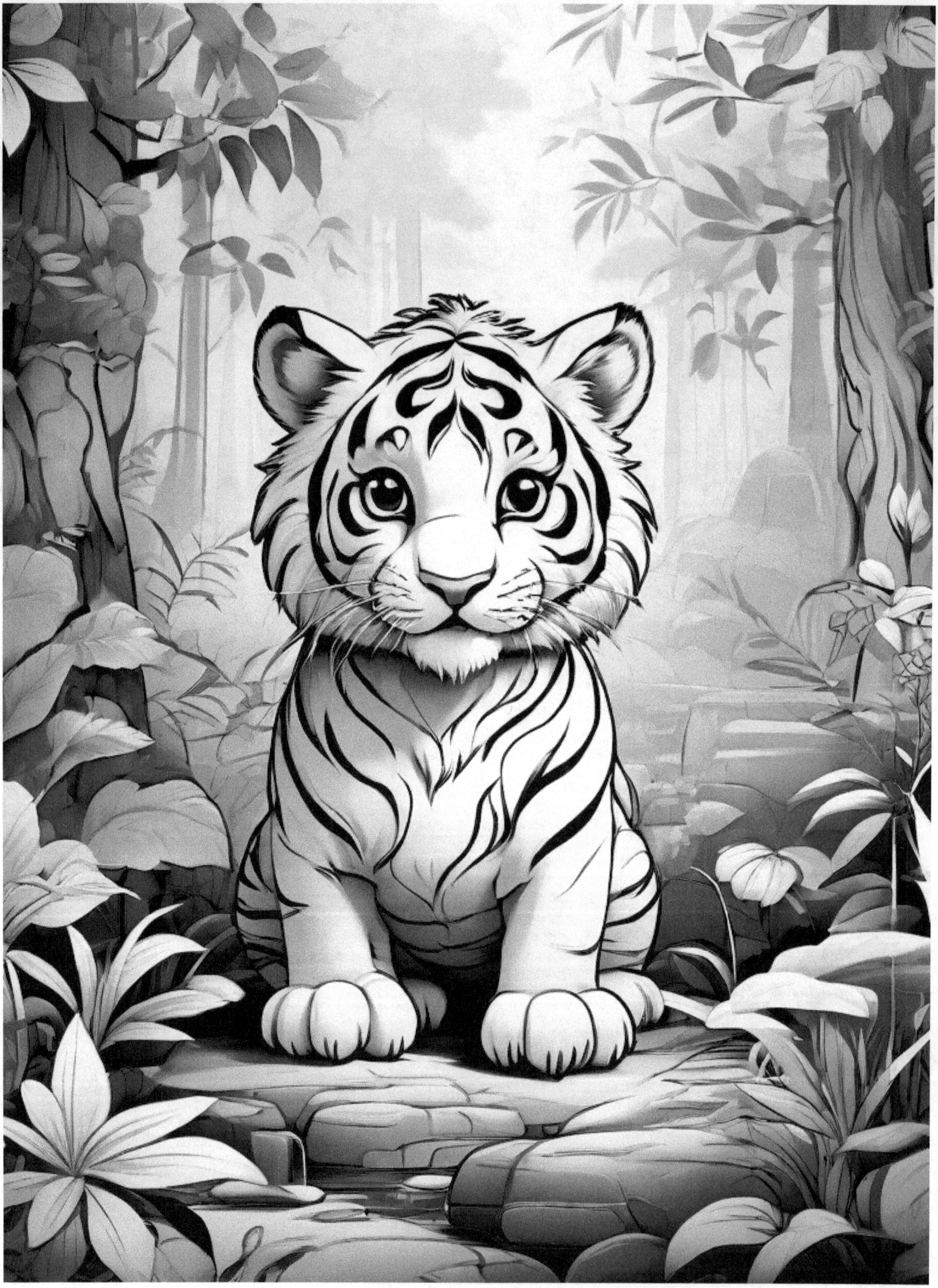

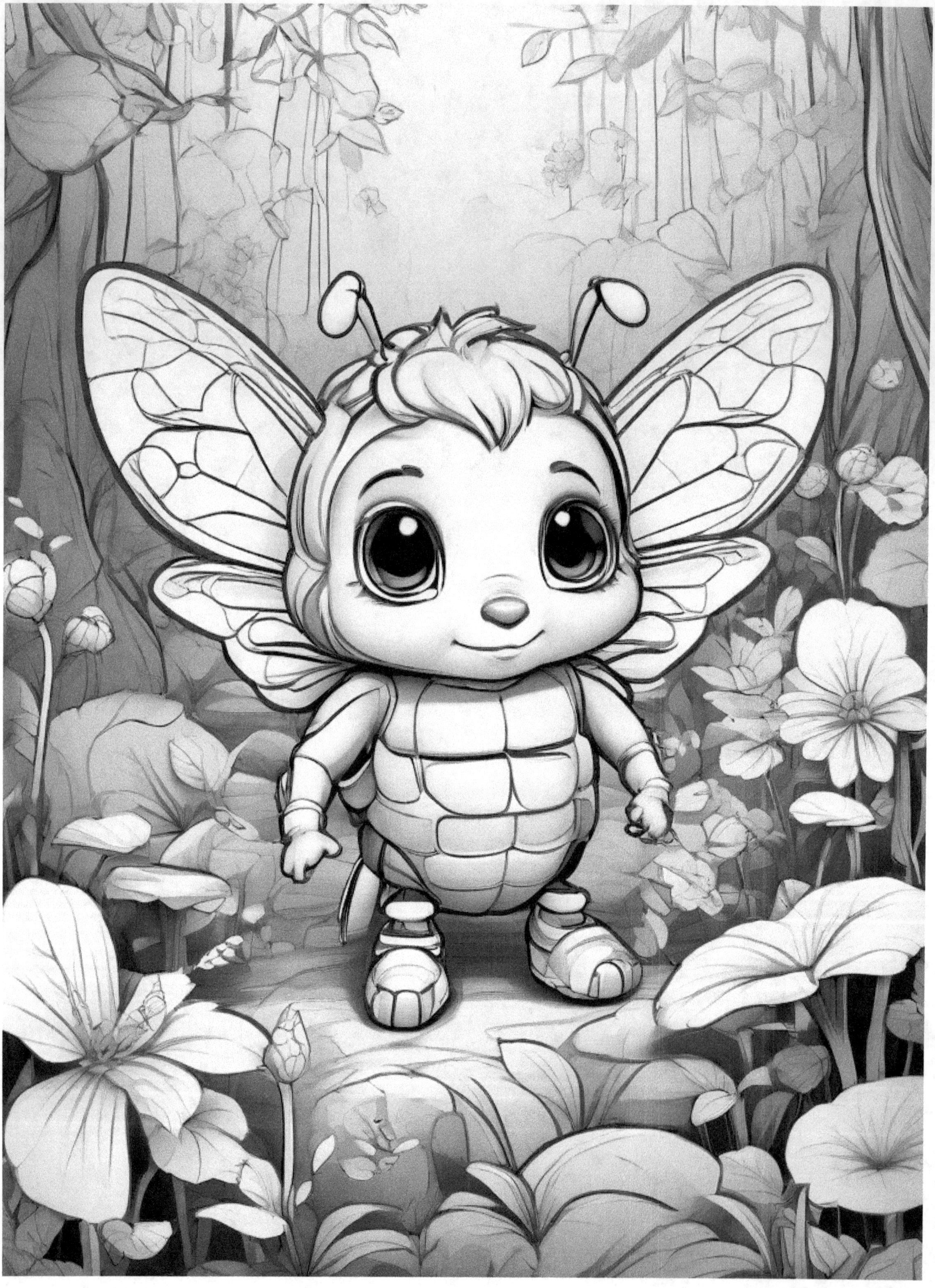

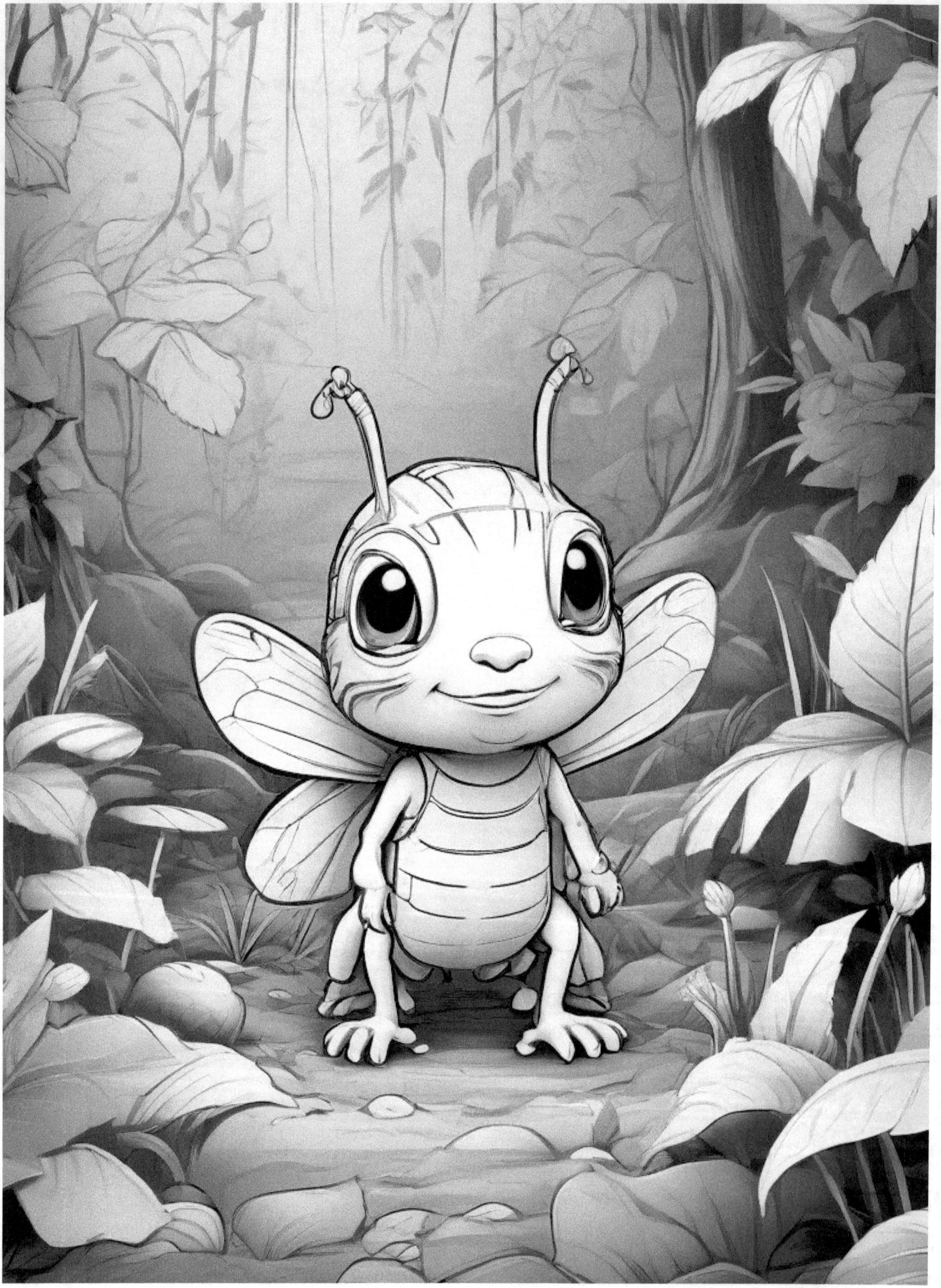

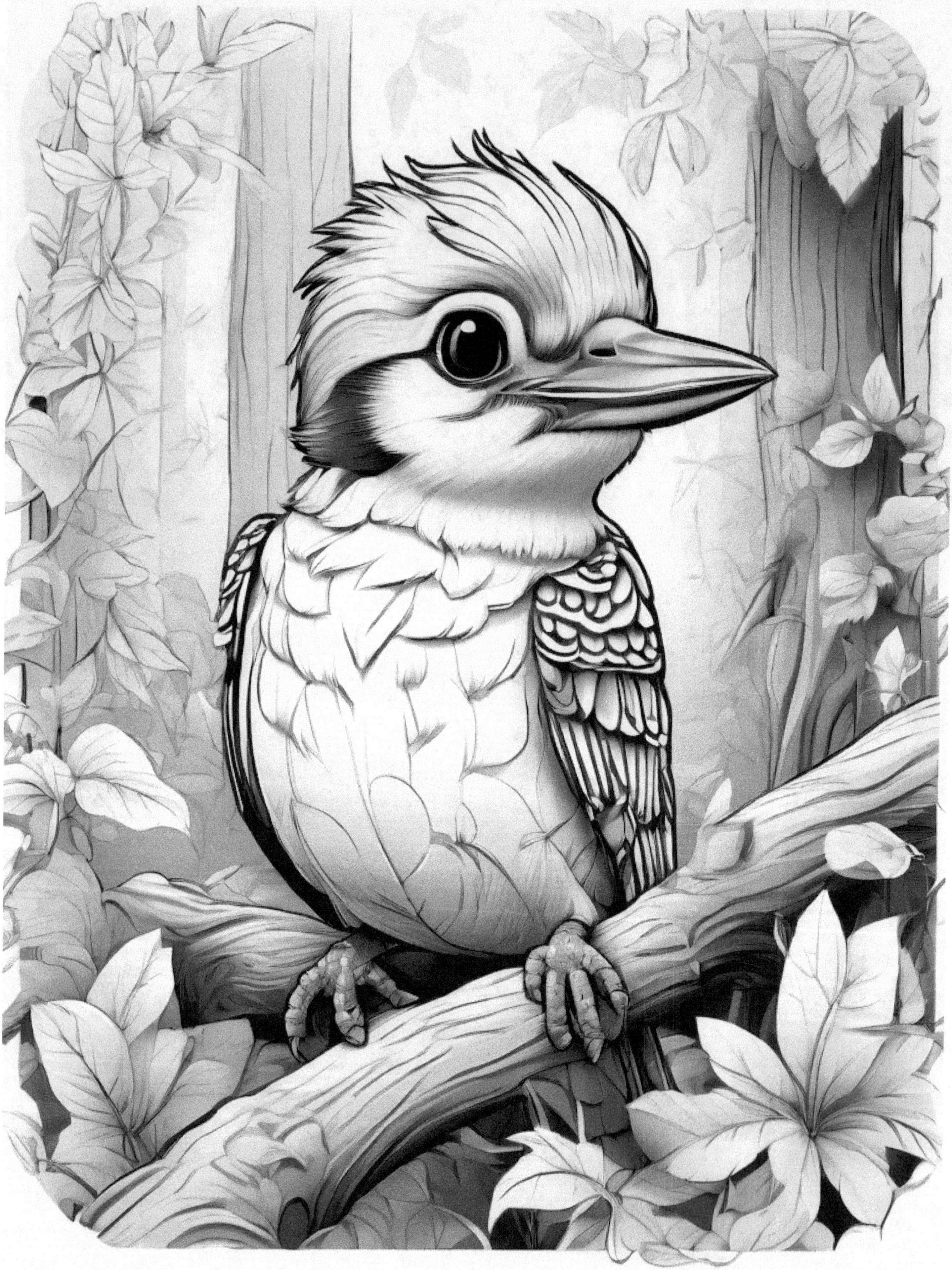

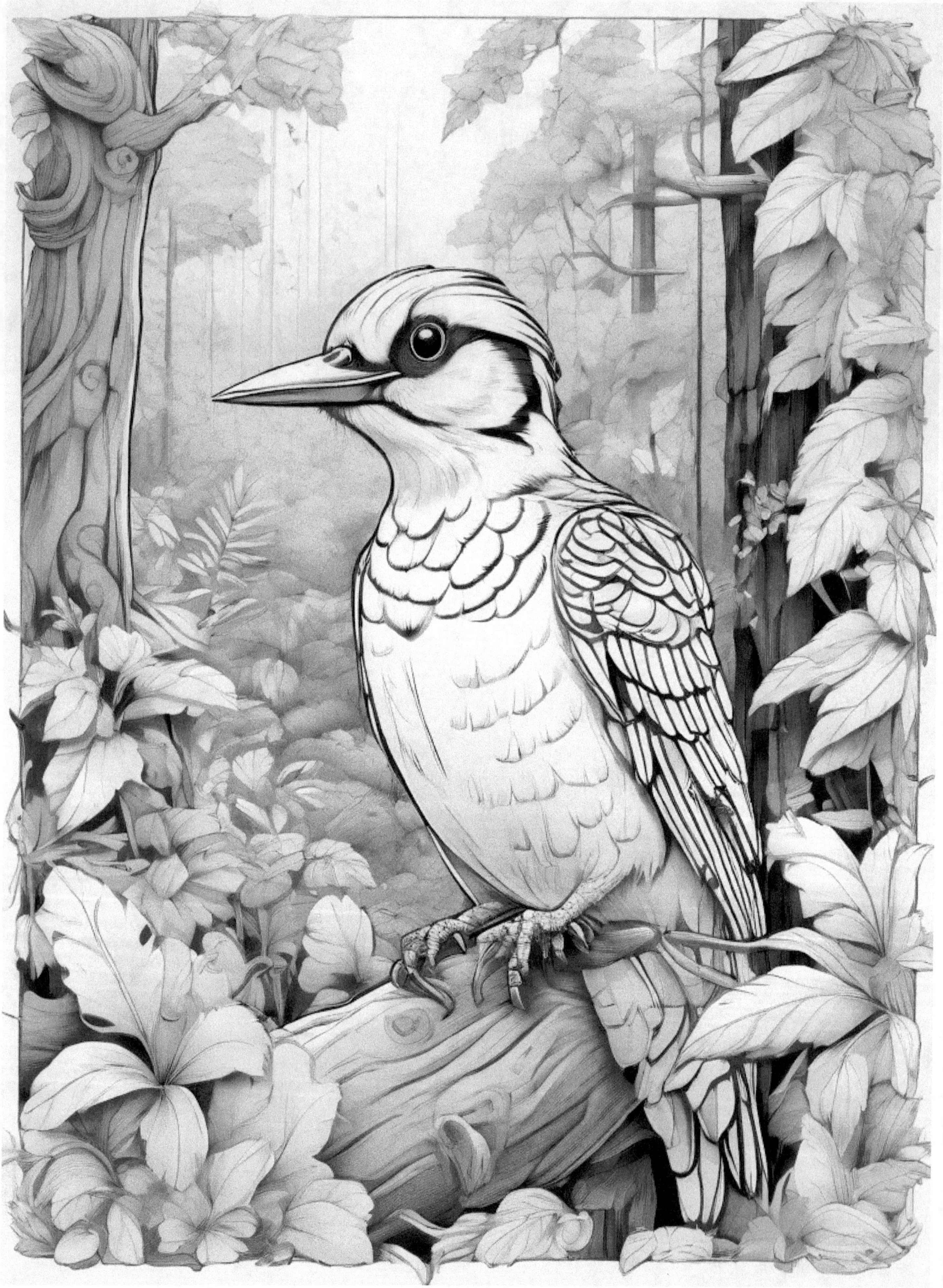

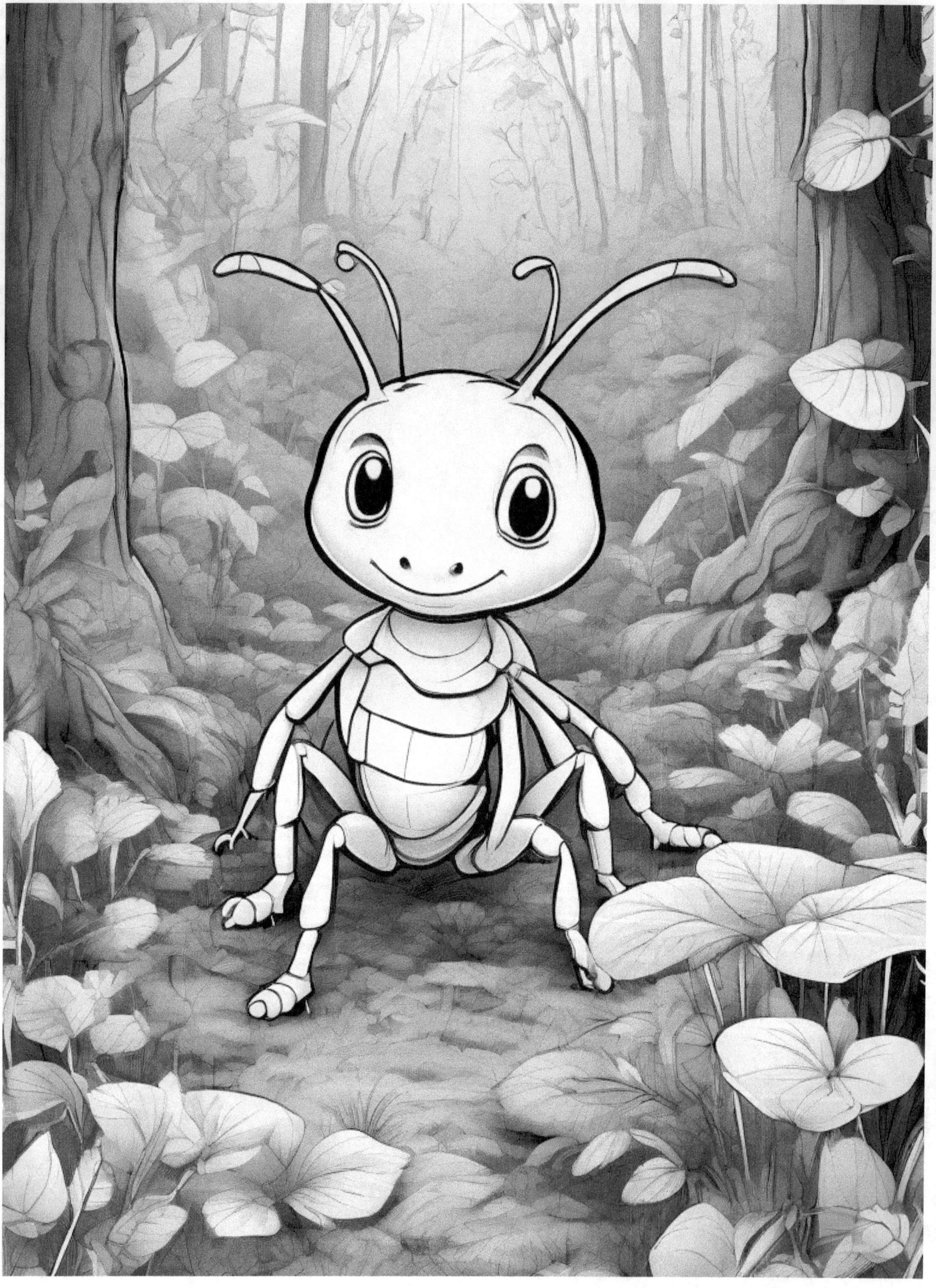

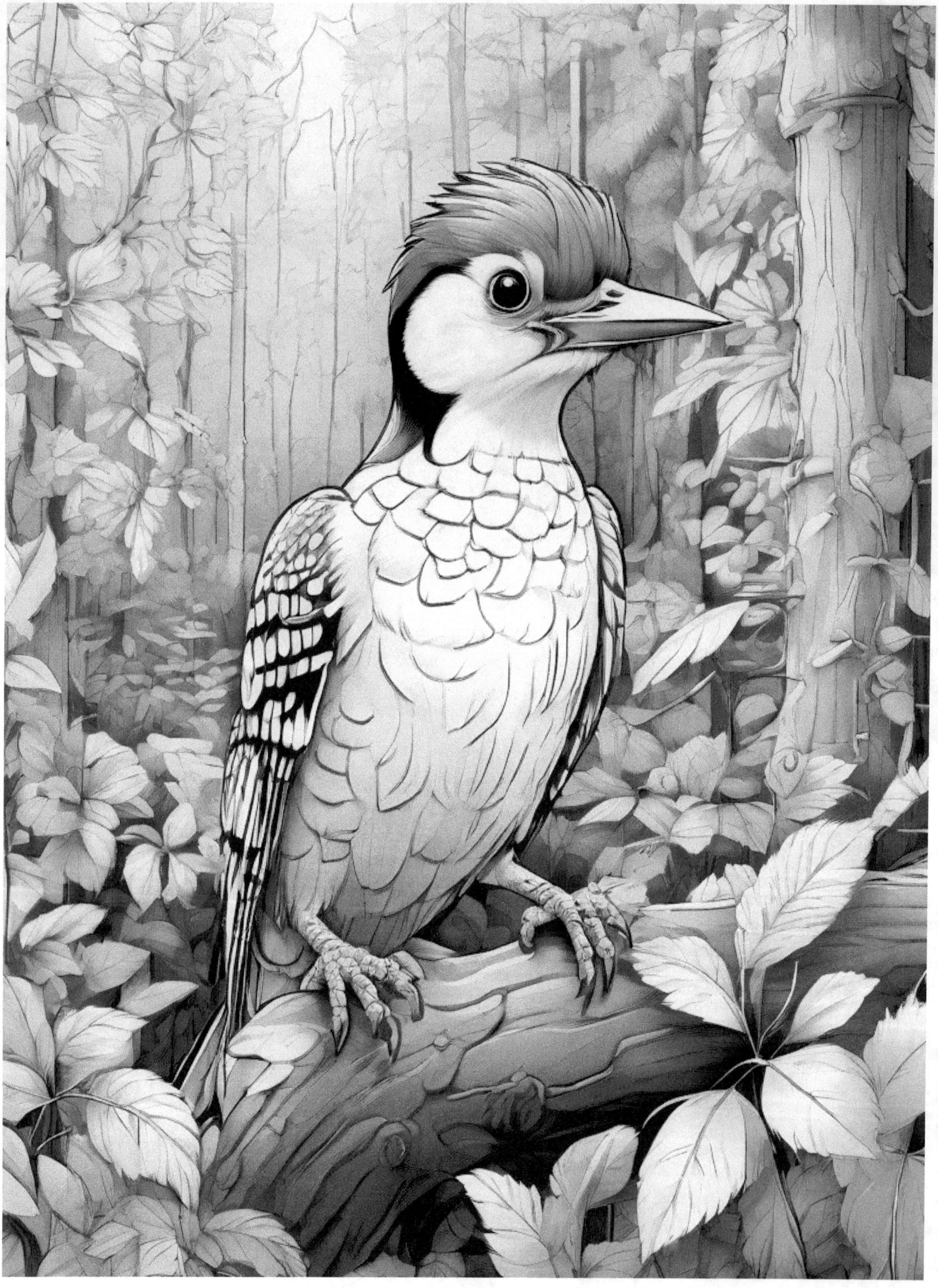

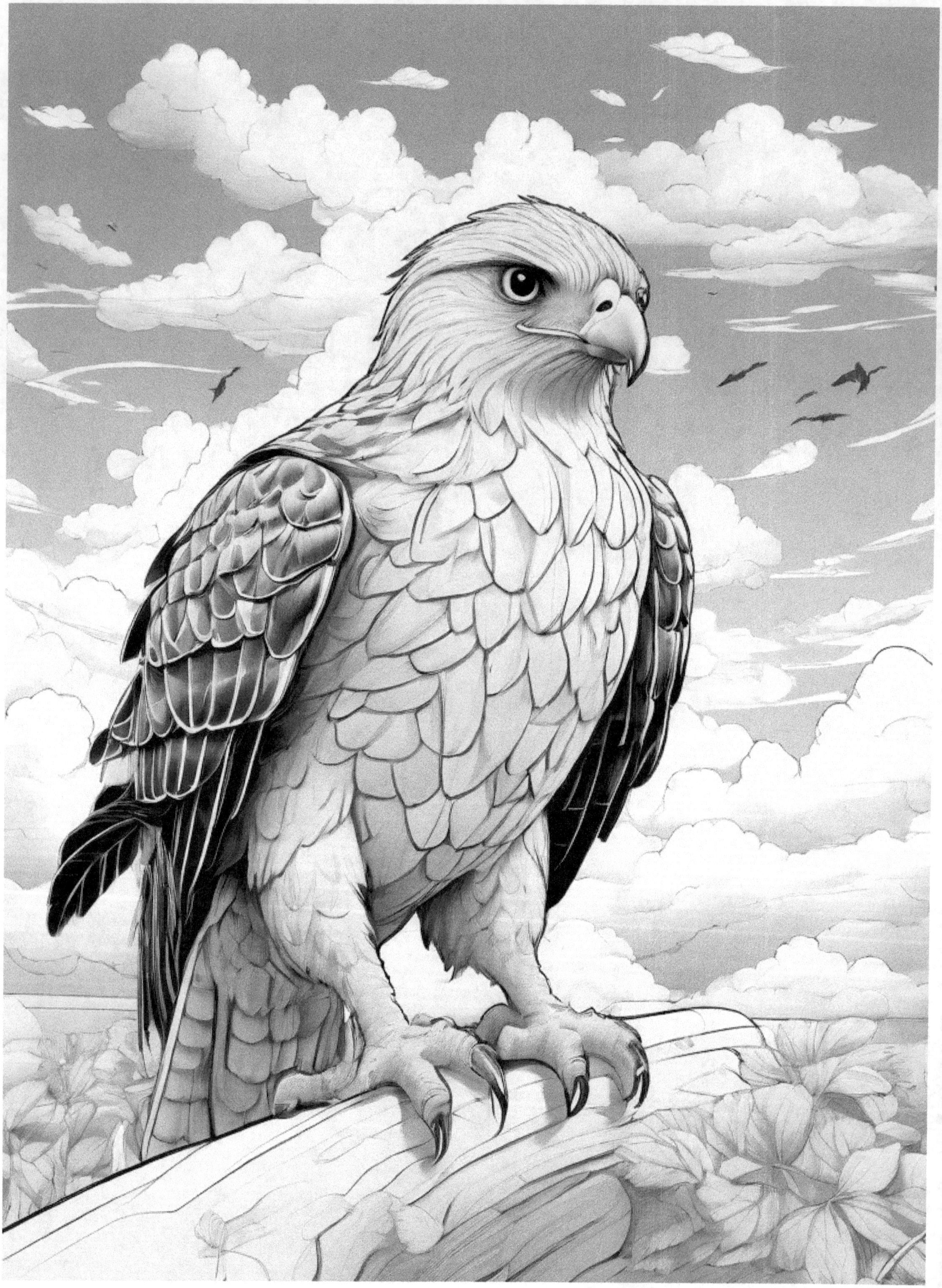

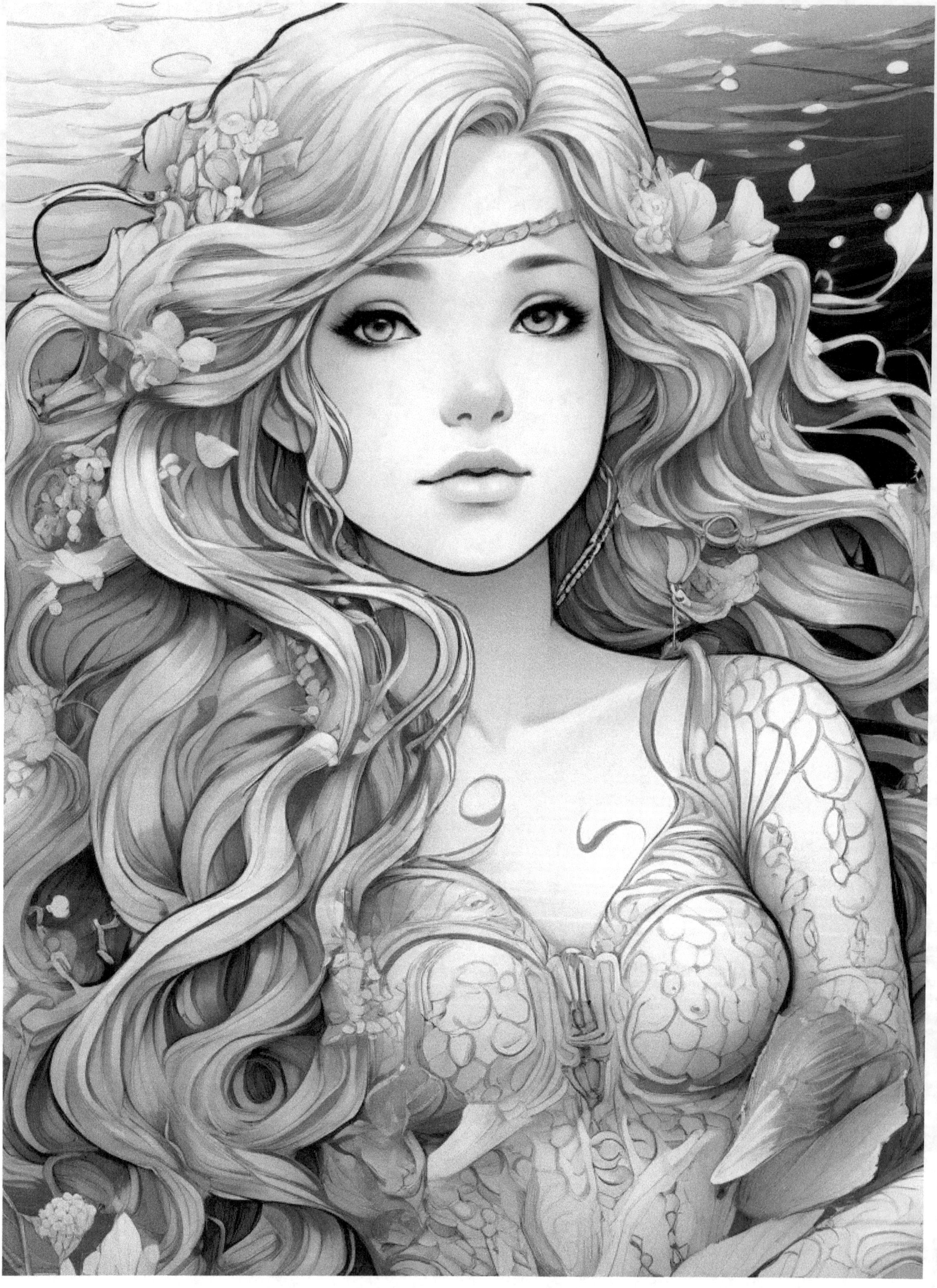

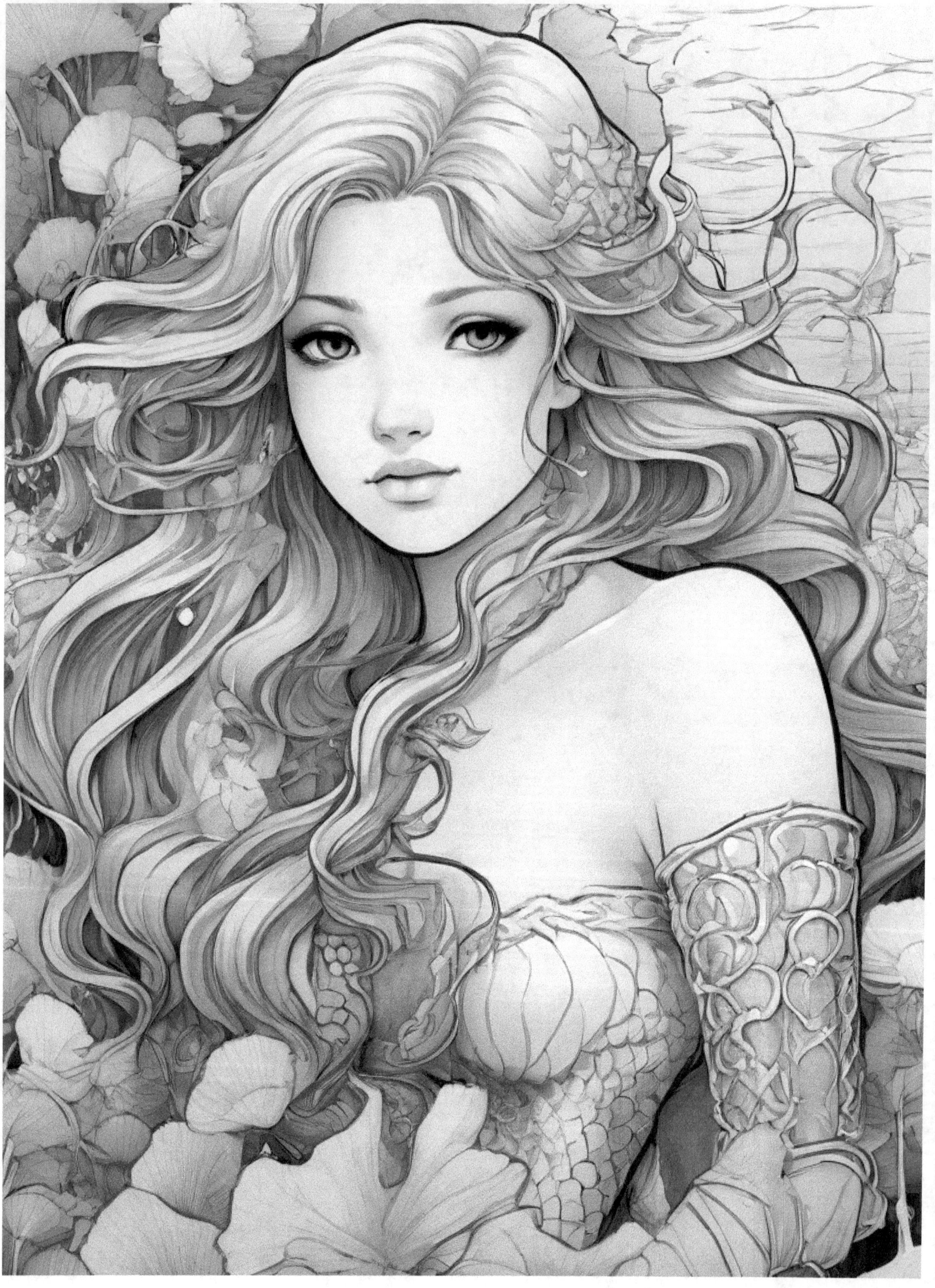

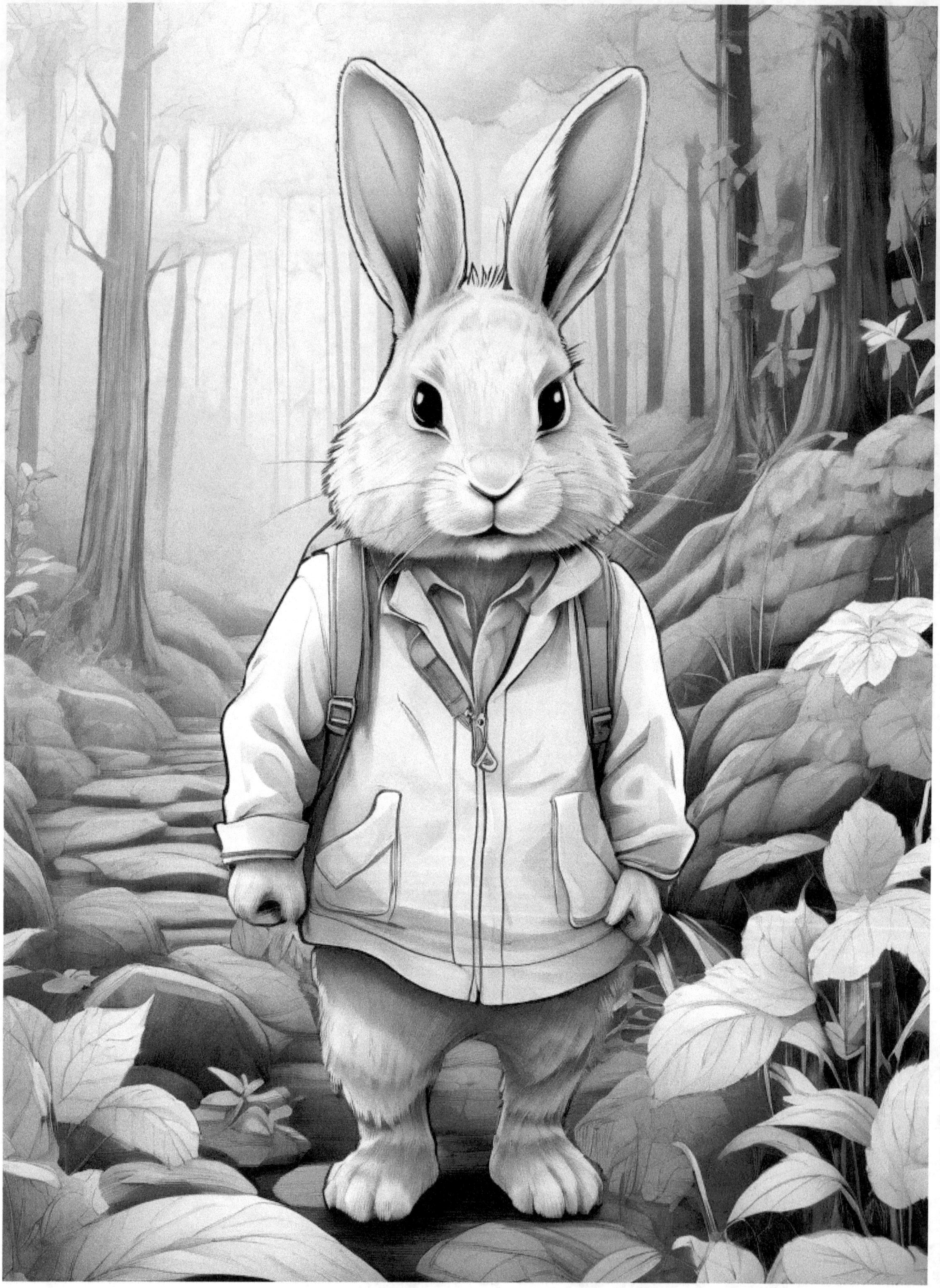

www.ingramcontent.com/pod-product-compliance
Lightning Source LLC
Chambersburg PA
CBHW080941260726
48661CB00010B/4020
* 9 7 9 8 8 7 1 1 1 7 7 0 5 *